A Book Of

HUMAN RESOURCE MANAGEMENT

For

M.B.A. Semester - II
As Per New Revised Syllabus from June 2019
Choice Based Credit System and Grading System
Compulsory Generic Core Course

Dr. Shalaka Parker
M.A. (English), B.Ed., PGDM & MMS
Ph.D. – Management (UoP)
Dean of the MBA Program
D.Y. Patil Institute of Masters of
Computer Application and
Management, Akurdi, Pune

Dr. Ashutosh Zunjur
B.Pharm, MBA (Ph.D., SPPU)
Assistant Professor,
D.Y. Patil Institute of Masters of
Computer Application and
Management, Akurdi, Pune.

Mrs. Viral S. Ahire
B.Com, MBA (HRM)
Assistant Professor,
D.Y. Patil Institute of Masters of
Computer Application and
Management, Akurdi, Pune.

Mrs. Arati Oturkar
B.Sc., MCM, MBA (HR)
Assistant Professor,
Sankalp Business School, Pune.

N4783

MBA - Sem. II : Human Resource Management   **ISBN 978-93-89825-56-5**

First Edition : **January 2020**

© : **Authors**

Published By :

NIRALI PRAKASHAN

Abhyudaya Pragati, 1312, Shivaji Nagar,
Off J.M. Road, PUNE – 411005
Tel - (020) 25512336/37/39, Fax - (020) 25511379
Email : niralipune@pragationline.com

➤ DISTRIBUTION CENTRES

PUNE

Nirali Prakashan : 119, Budhwar Peth, Jogeshwari Mandir Lane, Pune 411002, Maharashtra
(For orders within Pune)   Tel : (020) 2445 2044, Mobile : 9657703145
Email : niralilocal@pragationline.com

Nirali Prakashan : S. No. 28/27, Dhayari, Near Asian College Pune 411041
(For orders outside Pune)   Tel : (020) 24690204 Fax : (020) 24690316; Mobile : 9657703143
Email : bookorder@pragationline.com

MUMBAI

Nirali Prakashan : 385, S.V.P. Road, Rasdhara Co-op. Hsg. Society Ltd.,
Girgaum, Mumbai 400004, Maharashtra; Mobile : 9320129587
Tel : (022) 2385 6339 / 2386 9976, Fax : (022) 2386 9976
Email : niralimumbai@pragationline.com

➤ DISTRIBUTION BRANCHES

JALGAON

Nirali Prakashan : 34, V. V. Golani Market, Navi Peth, Jalgaon 425001, Maharashtra,
Tel : (0257) 222 0395, Mob : 94234 91860; Email : niralijalgaon@pragationline.com

KOLHAPUR

Nirali Prakashan : New Mahadvar Road, Kedar Plaza, 1st Floor Opp. IDBI Bank, Kolhapur 416 012
Maharashtra. Mob : 9850046155; Email : niralikolhapur@pragationline.com

NAGPUR

Nirali Prakashan : Above Maratha Mandir, Shop No. 3, First Floor,
Rani Jhanshi Square, Sitabuldi, Nagpur 440012, Maharashtra
Tel : (0712) 254 7129; Email : niralinagpur@pragationline.com

DELHI

Nirali Prakashan : 4593/15, Basement, Agarwal Lane, Ansari Road, Daryaganj
Near Times of India Building, New Delhi 110002 Mob : 08505972553
Email : niralidelhi@pragationline.com

BENGALURU

Nirali Prakashan : Maitri Ground Floor, Jaya Apartments, No. 99, 6th Cross, 6th Main,
Malleswaram, Bengaluru 560003, Karnataka; Mob : 9449043034
Email: niralibangalore@pragationline.com

Other Branches : Hyderabad, Chennai

niralipune@pragationline.com | www.pragationline.com

Also find us on www.facebook.com/niralibooks

Preface/Foreword ...

In today's scenario, the concept of Human Resource which was primarily responsible for the administrative functions has been replaced by "Human Capital Management "concept. The Human Resource Management has widen its horizon and has conveyed in the idea of becoming a "Business Partner". In this cut throat competition many organizations are struggling to change various HR processes and technologies. And for this new thinking, new vision and a new mission is required to achieve the business success.

We are glad to present this book, especially designed to cater the needs of the MBA students and other readers. The book has been written keeping in mind the fundamental concepts of the HRM. The language of book is quite easy and understandable based on logical approach. It is based on the revised syllabus set by the University of Pune (SPPU) with effect from June 2019.

The structure of the book contains five major chapters which are as follows:

1. **Chapter 1:** It deals with various concepts and challenges of Human Resource Management.
2. **Chapter 2:** Explains Human Resource Acquisition and various strategies related to retention.
3. **Chapter 3:** Helps to manage the performance of employees by providing them various types of training in order to enhance their knowledge, skills and abilities.
4. **Chapter 4:** It deals with Compensation management.
5. **Chapter 5:** It is related with Emerging trends in Human resource management.

The book also contains skills based exercise as well as the case studies related to each and every chapter. Various figures will helps to understand the exact logic behind the most complicated topics. Any further improvement in the contents of the book by making corrections, omission and inclusion is keen to be achieved based on suggestions from the readers for which the authors shall be obliged.

We acknowledge special thanks to the Nirali Prakashan, Shri Jignesh Furia and the entire staff of Nirali Prakashan, Pune who have been constant source of motivation throughout this Endeavour. A very special thanks to Mr. Amol Mahabal for solving the queries related to the syllabus.

We also thank Mr. Malik Shaikh and Mrs. Yojana Deshpande for their valuable contribution in the preparation of this book.

We are sure that the book will be a good guidance to the students. As authors we are quite confident that this textbook will receive the patronage of all for whom it is intended.

Authors

Syllabus ...

1. **Human Resource Management - Concept and Challenges:**

   Introduction, Objectives, Scope, Features of HRM, Role of HRM, Importance of HRM, Policies and Practices of HRM, Functions of HRM, Challenges of HRM. Introduction to SHRM: Define SHRM, importance and nature. HRM Models: Harvard Model, SHRM "matching model". (5 + 2)

2. **HR Acquisition and Retention:**

   Human Resource Planning: Definition, Objective, Need and Importance, HRP Process, Barriers to HRP. Job Analysis Process – Contents of Job Description and Job Specification, Job description Vs job specification, Job design, Factors affecting Job design, Job enrichment Vs job enlargement. Recruitment: Introduction and Sources of Recruitment, Difference between recruitment and selection-Recruitment, Selection Process, Induction and Orientation. Career Planning-Process of career planning and development, Succession Planning Process, Transfer and Promotion. Retention of Employees: Importance of retention, strategies of retention. (8 + 2)

3. **Managing Employee Performance and Training:**

   Performance Appraisal and Performance Management – Definition, Objective, Importance, Appraisal Process and Appraisal Methods. Why to measure performance and its purpose. Performance Appraisal Vs Performance Management, Potential Management. Training and Development - Definition – Scope – Conceptual framework of Training and development of Employees, Role of Training in Organizations, Objectives, The Training and Development Process, Training Need Assessment, Types of training, Difference between training and development, E-Learning. Benefits of training, Evaluation of Training Effectiveness: Kirkpatrick model. (8 + 2)

4. **Compensation Management:**

   Concept, Objectives, Importance of Compensation Management, Process, Current Trends in Compensation. Factors in compensation plan. Wage / Salary differentials, Components of salary. Incentives and Benefits – Financial and Non-financial Incentive, Fringe Benefits. Employees Separation – Retirement, Termination, VRS, Golden Handshake, Suspension, Concepts and Methods, Grievance Procedure in Indian Industry. (8 + 2)

5. **Emerging Trends in HRM:**

   HRIS - Need, Advantages and Uses of HRIS. HR Accounting- Concepts, Objective, Advantage, Limitation and Method. HR Audit - Concept, Objective, Scope and Process. HR Shared Services - Concept, Objective, Benefits, Issues creating HR Shared Services. (6 + 2)

***

Contents ...

***

Human Resource Management : Concept and Challenges

Contents ...

Learning Objectives:

- ➢ Understand the meaning of Human Resource Management.
- ➢ Define the Objectives, Scope, Features and Role of Human Resource Management.
- ➢ Examine the various challenges faced by Human Resource Management.
- ➢ Understand the Concept of Strategic Human Resource Management.
- ➢ Understand Models of Human Resource Management as well as Strategic Human Resource Management.

Opening Vignettes/Pragmatic Insight: Infosys Technologies has achieved the "***Best Employer of the Year***" by a number of leading Human Resource Surveys for its outstanding HR practices. It is one of those companies who has not only successfully altered the attitude and behaviour of the employees but also the performance of the organization through creative HR practices. The HR policies of Infosys include:

(1) To focus on learning ability of candidate at the time of recruitment.

(2) To impart continuous learning through employee training.

For this reason it has developed a World Class Training Center called as "Global Education Center in Mysore to train the fresh talent and an "Infosys Leadership Institute" to develop the future leaders of the organization.

(3) To evaluate the performance of the employees on continuous basis through competency mapping system, and

(4) To use the best compensation structure which considers the collective performance of an individual, the team and the organization as a whole for fixing the employee compensation packages.

To conclude, its HR philosophy, policies, practices and management have played a pivotal role in making Infosys the best company in the entire world.

"You must treat your employees with respect and dignity because in the most automated factory in the world, you need the power of human mind. That is what brings in innovation. If you want high quality minds to work for you, then you must protect the respect and dignity. "- **Mr N.R. Narayana Murthy, Infosys Ltd.**

The success story of Infosys is itself a proof the Human Resource Management (HRM) can be a definite competitive advantage for the firm and can make a real difference not only to the richness of the organization but also to the individuals as well. Keeping this success story in mind, let us first get acquainted with the basics of HRM in this chapter.

1.1 Introduction to Human Resource Management

Every organization is essentially a combination of physical and human resources (HR). Physical resources refer to materials, men, machines set by the organization for production or trade,while Human resources on the other hand refers to knowledge, skills, abilities and expertise of the members of the organization. All the resources of the organization are equally important for the achievement of the objectives of an organization. In fact, the effectiveness of any organization lies in the judicious merger of the two resources to achieve optimum competency.

However for the long time it was felt that the efficient utilization of physical resources was the foremost part for developing any organization. This was because the acquisition of physical resources resulted in a huge outflow of funds and those assets which carried an exact value. On the contrary, it was felt that hiring employees never cost anything significant for a firm and it was quite easy to replace them. This made the importance less for the human resources in the mind of employers.

But in the past decades, employers have realized that intellectual capital is critical to business success. The main reasons for this change are due to the understanding that:

1. Innovation of the product and Marketing tactics are important to survive in the market as well as growth in competitive environment is possible only when a good and inventive workforce is present.

2. People are not alike and are not treated identically. They differ physically and mentally. These differences require individual attention in order to achieve the finest productivity.

3. Human resources are the only assets which appreciate over a period, while physical resources just depreciate with years.

Indian organizations are no exception to this change in understanding. They realized that technology itself is not only sufficient to conquer the market but along with technology we need efficient workforce for the success of an organization. Organizations are managed by people and through people. Without people, organizations never exist. In fact people are the only one who makes the company with their uniqueness but also on the same time they break the company. With the growing importance of Human resources in the organization, its management became one of the most important part in order to retain good skill and talent.

1.2 Definitions of Human Resource Management

- *Dale Yoder Defines* *"Manpower management effectively describes the process of planning and directing the application, development and utilization of human resources in employment".*

- *Michael Jucius defines Human resource as "Human Factor"* *which is a whole consisting of inter-related, inter-dependent and interacting physiological, psychological, sociological and ethical components."*

- *Edwin Flippo defines*- *Human Resource Management as "planning, organizing, directing, controlling of procurement, development, compensation, integration, maintenance and separation of human resources to the end that individual, organizational and social objectives are achieved."*

- *Decenzo and Robbins defines* *"Human Resource Management is concerned with the people dimension in management. Since every organization is made up of people, acquiring their services, developing their skills, motivating them to higher levels of performance and ensuring that they continue to maintain their commitment to the organization is essential to achieve organsational objectives. This is true, regardless of the type of organization – government, business, education, health or social action".*

- ***The National Institute of Personal Management (NIPM) of India defines Human Resources – Personal Management as*** *"that part of management which is concerned with people at work and with their relationship within an enterprise. Its aim is to bring together and develop into an effective organization of the men and women who make up enterprise and having regard for the well – being of the individuals and of working groups, to enable them to make their best contribution to its success".*

1.3 Objectives of Human Resource Management

The primary objective of the HRM is to take care of the employees i.e. its workforce from the time they enter into the organization to the time they leave it, while ensuring the best possible support in achieving the organizational goals and objectives.

The Objectives of HRM can be classified into the following:

1. To help the organization to attain its goals effectively and efficiently by providing competent and motivated employees.
2. To utilize the available human resources effectively.
3. To act as a liaison between the top management and the employees.
4. To increase to the fullest the employee's job satisfaction and self-actualization.
5. To develop and maintain the quality of work life.
6. To reconcile individual group goals with organizational goals
7. To devise employee benefit schemes for improving employee motivation and group morale and enhance employer-employee cooperation.

Pragmatic Insights describe the HR Objectives of the Reliance Group:

"In my book, we have no greater asset than the quality of our intellectual capital, and no greater priority than the growth and retention of our vast pool of talent".

– Anil Dhirubhai Ambani

Reliance Group shall always recognize the critical role played by its people for the success and growth of business. It is their skill, initiative; commitment and dedication that lends us the competitive edge, and helps us stay ahead of the curve. They provide equal growth opportunities to all its employees irrespective to their race, caste, religion, color, origin, marital status, gender, sexual orientation, age, nationality, ethnic origin or disability in order to expand their leadership capabilities. They believe in true meritocracy and also freedom to choose their career paths.

Employees of Reliance Group are provided with the opportunities to develop and hone leadership and functional capabilities in order to achieve their personal and organizational goals. They are provided with an entrepreneurial environment where each and every employee can pursue their dreams. They also provide a well-defined Rewards and Recognitions programme that periodically identifies exceptional individual and team achievers among the various business functions and verticals in the Group which directly helps in maintaining a work environment free of all forms of harassment, whether physical, verbal or psychological.

(Adapted from:https://www.relianceada.com/human-resources)

1.4 Scope of Human Resource Management

The scope of HRM is wide. An understanding of HRM is important to anyone who works in an organization. Issues related to HR become important whenever there is group of workers. The scope of HRM consists of acquisition, development, maintenance/retention, and control of human resources in the organization **(See below figure 1.1)**.

Acquisition: Human Resource Planning, Recruitment, Selection, Placement

Development: Training, Organizational Development, Career Development and Internal Mobility

Scope of HRM

Maintenance: Remuneration, Motivation, Health and Safety, Social Security, Industrial Relations. Performance Appraisal.

Control: Human Resource Audit, Human Resource Accounting, Human Resource Information System.

Fig. 1.1: Scope of HRM

The National Institute of Personnel Management, Kolkatta has specified the scope of HRM as follows:

1. **The Labour or Personnel Aspect:** This is concerned with manpower planning, recruitment, selection, placement, transfer, promotion, training and development, lay-off and retrenchment, remuneration, incentives, productivity, etc.

2. **Welfare Aspect:** It deals with working conditions, and amenities such as canteen, creches, rest and lunch rooms, housing, transport, medical assistance, education, health and safety, recreation facilities, etc.

3. **Industrial Relations Aspects:** This covers union-management relations, joint consultation, collective bargaining, grievance and disciplinary actions, settlement of disputes, etc.

1.5 Features of Human Resource Management

According to V. P. Michael, *the feature of the human resource management is to "reflect a new philosophy, a new outlook, approach and strategy, which views an organization's manpower as its resources and assets and not as liabilities or mere hands". Thus, human resource or manpower is considered today to be the vital resource to develop the organization.*

Some of the important features and characteristics of human resource management are:

1. **Universal Force:** HRM is universal in nature as it is present in all the organizations. It is applicable at all levels of the management in an organization. As a matter of fact, HRM is closely associated with the strategic decision making process of the organization involving all departments and functions in the organization. Thus even for Small Enterprise, Entrepreneur should have knowledge of HRM which would help him successfully managing his people in the organization.

2. **Decision Oriented:** HRM mainly focuses on decisions rather than keeping records of all the necessary details which was used long back as traditional method in personnel management practices. Decisions in HRM mainly includes performance improvement through further training, or a promotion based on satisfactory performance by an employee.

3. **Focus on Individual needs and objectives:** HRM emphasis more on identifying individual needs and objectives by analyzing his capabilities through various analysis. Hence it makes an attempt to improve further an individual and encourage them to give their best to the organization.

4. **Employee Oriented:** HRM is concerned about people. It mainly deals and revolves around the capabilities of the people rather than the individual. Thus the paradigm shift had been from assigning people allotted tasks in order to utilize knowledge and human capabilities for higher performance outcomes in an organization.

5. **Development and Growth Oriented:** Development is an initiative taken by an organization to acquire better work related skills and behaviours. In the context where organizations are emphasizing more upon sharing and developing knowledge, the concept of development attains a wider or broader meaning in terms of realizing the capabilities of people/rather knowledge workers. It focuses on the holistic development of people with in collaboration with various strategies ensuring the acquisition of the desired behaviour and capabilities among people. The reward and incentive structures should be fine-tuned along with the development oriented concept.

6. **Employees - An Internal Customers:** HRM is mainly responsible for treating their employees as the "internal customers" of the organization. In this perspective HR professionals need to play various roles in several other functional domains of their organization such as logistics, finance, supply chain management, total quality management, marketing and corporate relations in order smoothen organizational effectiveness.

7. **Strategic Implications:** In today's highly competitive business environment, HRM should assume the role of the strategic decision maker in the organization. HR professionals in this regard need to shoulder the responsibility of being the strategic partners of the business and help the organization to successfully in achieving their business objectives by aligning people to the strategic goals of the organization.

8. **Support Functions:** The HR function of an organization is service oriented. HRM not only just accomplish their administrative or HR-related work more effectively, but also provide session as internal consultants and extend "subject-matter-expert (SME)" help and assistances whenever required. HR activities like Talent tracking, Reward management are examples of the Service function.

9. **Multi-disciplinary Nature:** HRM is a multi-disciplinary in nature. It includes knowledge and from various disciplines and studies like those of psychology, sociology, anthropology, political science, economics, quantitative techniques and statistical applications, econometrics, ergonomics (Quality of life and work environment designing), financial concepts (Human resource accounting and HR-audit) etc. The multi-disciplinary aspect of HR function, helps HR professionals to work as a strategic partners as well as internal consultants of the organization.

10. **Ongoing and Forward Looking Nature:** HRM is an ongoing process that starts at the strategic level in the organization and transfers into each and every functional domain of the organization. Today's HR practices are mostly forward looking and they constantly take into consideration the future needs and requirements of the business.

1.6 Role of Human Resource Management

Human Resources Management plays a critical role in an organization. It plays a crucial role in process of converting inputs into outputs, product design, quality maintenance, rendering services and many other functions which depend largely on the human efficiency. There are Six main role played by Human Resources Management in an organization. **They are mainly shown in Figure 1.2.**

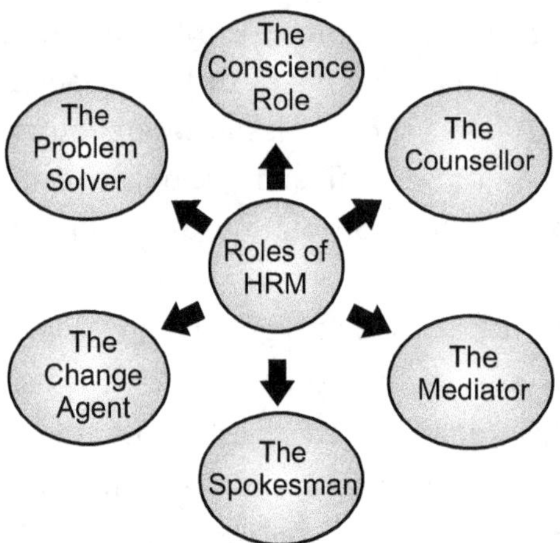

Fig. 1.2: Roles of HRM

1. **The Conscience Role:** HR manager plays an important role of reminding the management its morals and obligations towards its employees.

2. **The Counsellor:** An important role of the HR manager is that of a counsellor. If an employee is dissatisfied with the job he approaches to the HR manager for counselling and guidance in the area where he founds any problems related to his personal/professional life which he feels may influence his performance. Here the HR manager hears his problems and offer solution related to it.

3. **The Mediator:** In any organization there are times where a person experiences many misunderstanding between management and employees or between employees themselves. So Here, HR manager acts as a Mediator, a Peace-maker and a Communication link between them.

4. **The Spokesperson:** HR manager acts as a spokesperson within the company, as well as are representative of the company.

5. **The Change Agent:** Change is something always resisted by the employees. HR manager acts as a change agent in order to bring about a change on the existing system or an introduction of a new system.

6. **Problem Solver:** HR manager acts as a problem solver with respect to the issues that involve human resources management and over all long range organizational planning.

1.7 Importance of Human Resource Management

Human Resource Management is the valuable assets of any organization. They are the pillars on the basis of which an organization accepts the new challenges. It can be seen in terms of three contexts such as:

(1)   Organizational,

(2)   Social,

(3)   Professional.

(1) Organizational Context:

HRM is of vital importance to the individual organization as a means for achieving their objectives. It contributes to the achievement of organizational objectives in the following ways:

➢   Good HR practices helps in retaining and attracting people in the organization.

➢   It also helps in developing essential skills and attitudes among the employees through Training and Development and Performance Appraisal.

➢   It helps in secure willing cooperation of employees through motivation, active participation, grievance handling etc.

➢   It ensures effective utilization of available human resources in an organization.

➢   It also confirms that enterprise will have in future a team of competent and dedicated employees.

(2) Social Context:

Social significance of HRM lies in the need satisfaction of personnel in the organization which directly contributes to the welfare of the society. Society, as a whole, is the major beneficiary of good human resource practice.

➢   Helps in multiplying employment opportunities at various extents.

➢   It also eliminates waste of human resources through conservation of physical and mental health.

➢   It makes sure that scare talents are put to best use. Companies that pay and treat people well always race ahead of others and deliver excellent results.

(3) Professional Context:

It lies in developing people and providing healthy environment for effective utilization of their capabilities. This is possible only when:

➢   Developments of people are done on continuous basis.

➢   Promotion of team work and team spirit are done in actual manner.

➢   Opportunities are provided to people with high talent and should have potential to prove them in the market.

➢   Organization provided healthy environment and equal opportunities to expose their creativity.

1.8 Functions of Human Resource Management

As Per Armstrong (1997) "Human resource management is defined as "a strategic approach to acquiring, developing, managing, motivating and gaining the commitment of the organization's key resource — the people who work in and for it."

In general, HRM is concerned with hiring, motivating and maintaining workforce within businesses.

Functions of Human Resource Management Includes:

Functions of Human Resource Management	
Managerial Functions	**Operative Functions**
• Planning	• Recruitment/Hiring
• Organizing	• Development
• Staffing	• Compensation
• Directing	• Maintenance and Motivation
• Controlling	• Integration

Managerial Functions includes:

1. **Planning:** It is one of the effective tool to deal with the future. It is one of the primary function which determine number and types of employees needed to accomplish organizational objectives. Here accurate forecasting plays vital role for the success of any plan. It is such a crucial function for an organization that is key to all managerial functions.

2. **Organizing:** Once the plans are formulated the next step is proper organization of the men and material in order to accomplish those plans. It is the process through which the firm establishes its structure and determines the authority, responsibility and accountability of each member in relation to the job.

3. **Staffing:** It deals with the creation and maintenance of human resources through employment, compensation, benefits, training and development and industrial relations measures. It aims to put in frame various HR policies in order to deal with wage fixation, working conditions and promotional opportunities for employees.

4. **Directing:** This includes activating employees at different levels and making them contribute maximum towards organizational goal. It aims at securing willing co-operation from the individuals and the groups to achieve the pre-determined goals.

5. **Controlling:** It is the process of checking the efficiency of the individuals and the groups in fulfilling the plans and goals through follow-up measures which is essential for continuous improvement in managerial activities.

Operational Functions includes:

1. **Recruitment/Hiring:** It refers to series of activities taken by HR managers to fulfill the present and future vacancies of the organization. Activities such as Job Analysis and designing, HR planning, Recruitment and finally the Selection of the suitable employees are included.

2. **Development:** It refers to both employees training and management development. HR managers are responsible for conducting various training and development programmes for employees in order to increase their competencies in their job by improving their KSA's (Knowledge, Skills, Abilities).

3. **Compensation:** Compensation refers to determine the pay scale and other benefits for the employees. To establish good pay policies in organization enhance the efficiency of employees. It is also one of the primary job of HR manager. They must make sure that their employees get fair and equitable pay rates. In addition, HR managers should regularly manage the performance evaluation system of the organization and continuously design reward system such as performance based incentive plans, bonus, and flexible work schedules.

4. **Maintenance and Motivation:** It aims at retaining efficient and experienced employees in the organization. This calls for creative HR practices. Minimizing employee turnover and sustaining best performing employees within the organization is the key. In this regards HR managers are responsible for offering a wide range of HR programmes covering safety, health promotion and physical fitness, canteen facilities, recreation activities, transportation progammes, employee suggestion schemes, career counseling and growth for creating a positive work environment.

5. **Integration:** It consists of mainly industrial relations and aims at ensuring good employer–employee relations. HR managers must ensure ethical and fair treatment in disciplinary action, grievance redressal and career management processes. They should also counsel the employees and the management to prevent and when necessary, resolve disputes over labor agreements or other labor relation issues.

2. Policies and Practices in Human Resource Management:

The dictionary meaning of "Policy" is "Plan of action" and "Plan" is a policy. Policy is a statement of overall objectives of the organization in the various areas with which its operations are concerned. Policies written may be given a wide circulation among the workers so that they may know the organizational objectives and help the management in achieving them. Policies serve as guide to action. Policies respond "what" and "why". The policy is regarded as "setting governing regulations" or "norms". It is the basis of control.

HR policies, procedures and practices establish a framework to help to manage people. They cover everything from how the business recruits its staff through to ensuring employees are clear about procedures, expectations and rules, are how managers can go about resolving issues if they arise.

- **Why it is important ?**
  - ➢ They help to develop company culture.
  - ➢ They help employees to understand what is expected from them.
  - ➢ They serve as a mirror to your business standards.
  - ➢ They provide guidance and tools for managers to assist with the management of employees.
  - ➢ They provide rules surrounding fairness, consistency and clarity.
  - ➢ They ensure that an employee meets its legal obligations in regards to employees.
  - ➢ They help to assimilate new staff members and bring them up to speed in the shortest amount of time.

- **How it helps HRM ?**
  - ➢ To have manuals, forms and procedures which will help HR managers to have easy access of any records?
  - ➢ It helps to clarify your organization's expectations through Employee handbooks and individual policies and procedures.
  - ➢ It also helps to develop robust HR policies, procedures and practices linked to your business and proven to deliver results.
  - ➢ It enables organizations to manage their own recruitment exercises through Recruitment processes and tools.
  - ➢ It gives valuable advice and guidance for best practice and proven practical HR strategies for all business sizes.
  - ➢ In order to continuously help organization to develop best practice audits.

Pragmatic Insight: Harsha and **Franklin** both are post graduates in management under different streams from same B-School. Both of them are close to each other from the college days itself and the same friendship is continuing in the organization too as they are placed in the same company, Hy-tech Technology Solutions. Harsha placed in HR department as employee counselor and Franklin in Finance department as key Finance executive. As per the grade is concerned both are at same level but when responsibility is concerned, Franklin is holding more responsibility being in core Finance.

By nature Harsha is friendly in nature and ready to help the needy. Franklin is silent in nature ready to help if approached personally and always a bit egoistic in nature. They have successfully completed 4 years in the organization. And management is very much satisfied with both of them as they are equally talented and constant performers. Harsha felt that nowadays Franklin is not like as he use to be in past. She noticed some behavioural changes with him. During general conversations she feels that Franklin is taunting her that she is famous among the employees in the organization on the other hand, he is not even recognized by fellow employees. One morning Mr. Mehta General Manager Hy-tech technology solutions shocked while go through the mail received from Franklin about his resignation. Mr. Mehta called Harsha immediately and discussed about the same as she is close to Franklin. By hearing the news Harsha got stunned and said that she do not know this before she also revealed here current experience with him. Mr. Mehta who do not want to lose both of them promised her that he will handle this and he won't allow Franklin to resign. In the afternoon Mr. Mehta took Franklin to Canteen to make him comfortable after some general discussion he starts on the issue. Franklin, after some hesitations opened his thinking in front of Mr. Mehta.

The problem of Franklin is (1) when he comes alone to canteen the people from other departments don't even recognize him but if he accompanied by Harsha he get well treated by others. (2) one day both of them entered the company together the security in the gate wished them but the next day when he came alone the same security did not do so. (3) Even in meetings held in the once the points raised by Harsha will get more value so many a times he keeps silent in the meeting. It happens to Franklin that he has to face such degradation in each day of work which totally disturbs him. Franklin also questioned that" Harsha and myself have same qualification, from same institute, passed out in the same year both with first class. We have same number of experience in this organization. More over the responsibilities with me are more valuable than that of Harsha. After all this things if I am been ignored or unrecognized by the fellow employees my ego does not allow me to continue here".

By listening this statement Mr. Metha felt that it is not going to be very difficult to stop his resignation. Mr. Mehta explained Franklin the reasons for such partial behaviour of the employees. After listening to Mr. Mehta Franklin said sorry for his reaction and ready to take back his resignation. And he called Harsha and spoke with like before.

Questions:

1. *Find the reason that Mr. Mehta would have given to Franklin.*

Solution for Case Study

Mr. Mehta listening to this case understood the situation and realized the reason behind the partial response given by the employees towards Franklin and Harsha. As Franklin said both Harsha and Franklin are passed out from same college in same year. Both of them joined the company together, both have same experience. Even in performance wise both stands in the same level i.e. both are constant performers and good performers. Franklin analyzed all the above said similarities between him and Harsha. He also stated that he holds more responsibility than that of Harsha. One thing Franklin did not notice or analyzed is the job profile of Harsha. It is true that Franklin holds more responsibility than that of Harsha but when it comes to direct interaction with employees, Harsha wins the employees attention in this aspect. Harsha being counselor in HR she faces the employees every day. She developed good rapport among the employees due to her friendly nature. She is always remembered by the employees whenever they face any problem as she gives good counseling and most of the times she suggest best solutions for such issues. Franklin though holding key position his profile does not allow him to interact with the employees. Though he has helping tendency he does only when someone approached him personally. As the employees of other departments do not have any relation with him they never approach him for help. Mr. Mehta having good experience understood these things when Franklin explained his problems one by one. Later he relates each situation, explained by Franklin with the above said reasons, and made Franklin understood the reality. Mr. Mehta said that the security in the gate or the employees in the canteen who recognized Harsha and not Franklin would have interacted with her during counseling or approached her for any issues. And as usual she would have counseled well or solved the issues of them that is the reason why they treat her and wish her whenever where ever they meet her. When it comes to the case of Franklin, they would have hardly met him or interacted with him.

3. Challenges of Human Resource Management:

Today every organizations have realize that human resource is the most valuable asset and are adopting policies like competence building, job rotation, performance linked pay, empowerment, etc. which promote the overall development of the human resources. Nowadays inputs are also given in the field of employee welfare and social security with increased post-retirement benefits like health insurance, provident fund, pension, etc. HR professionals are now playing pivotal role by acquiring, preparing and maintaining human resources for meeting various upcoming challenges in the world of booming technology.

There are number of human resource management challenges (HR Challenges) that need to be address i.e.; Environmental challenges, Organizational challenges and Individual challenges, etc. These challenges are not related to the single dimension; rather they are directed towards multi-dimensional issues which should be taken utmost care.

Following are the broad categories of the Human Resource Management challenges in the today's competitive world.

1. **Environmental Challenges:** It is related to the external forces that exist in the outside environment of an organization and can affect the performance of the management of the organization. These forces are almost out of control as they can be regarded as threats to management and should be handled in a proactive manner. They are Rapid Change in the environment, Work Force Diversity, Globalization, Laws and Legislation, Technology, Job and Family Roles, Lack of Skills etc.

2. **Organizational Challenges:** They are related to the factors which are inside the organization but can be controlled by the management of the organization to greater extent. The HR managers take notice of such emerging problems in advance and also take corrective measures before these would convert into serious issues. It includes competitive position and flexibility, organizational restructuring and issues of downsizing, the exercise of self-managed teams, development of suitable organizational culture etc.

3. **Individual Challenges:** The decisions related to the specific individual employees are included in the individual challenges of HRM. The organizational issues are also affected by the fact that how employees are treated within the organizations. The problems related to the individual level are Productivity, Empowerment, Brain drain, Ethics and Social responsibility, Job insecurity and matching people with organization.

Thus a prudent understanding and efficient management of these challenges are pre-requisites if HRM is to add considerable value, show business results, enact professionalism and reveal fresh competencies in future.

4. **Introduction to Strategic Human Resource Management:**

Before defining SHRM let us first understand 'What Strategic Management is'?

Formulation, implementation and evaluation of Business Strategies (Policies) to accomplish organizational goals are significant steps involved in Strategic Management. Decisions pertaining to strategic management are taken by organization's top managers on behalf of owners of the organization. Business environment; in which any particular organization is functioning, keeps on changing continuously. Therefore organizations have to evaluate their strategies continuously so as to remain competitive in the business environment. The strategic management helps organization to assess its position in the industry, plan strategies, execute them and evaluate the effectiveness of strategies so implemented.

"Strategic Management is a manner by which organization plans to deal with the various aspects of management like problem perception, divergent thinking, substantial resources, decision making, innovations, taking risks, and facing uncertainty"- Cunningham.

Having understood the concept of Strategic Management in brief let us now get introduced to Strategic HRM.

1.9 Definitions of Strategic Human Resource Management

Strategic Human Resource Management is *the process of attracting, developing, rewarding, and retaining sound employees for the benefit of employees as individuals and organization as a whole.*

According to Miles and Snow *"Strategic Human Resource Management system that is tailored to the demands of the business strategy".*

According to Wright and McMahan, *"Strategic Human Resource Management is the pattern of planned human resource activities intended to enable an organization to achieve its goals".*

According to Schuler Jackson and Storey, *"By Strategic we mean that Human Resource activities should be systematically designed and intentionally linked to an analysis of the business and its context".*

While satisfying needs of organization, SHRM is equally responsible to satisfy needs of employees as individuals. To accomplish organizational goals through effective human resource practices; Human Resource (HR) Department of organization must work in close association with other departments. HR Department must have to interact and communicate with various other departments to understand their needs and objectives. Once these needs and objectives are understood; HR department then formulate strategies pertaining to Human Resource that align with those objectives and those of the organization as well. This, therefore results in reflection of the goals of organization in those of human resource department.

Earlier strategic HR function was perceived as necessity for legal compliance or compensation only; but now it is considered as partner in success of the organization. Strategic Human Resource Management makes other departments stronger and more effective utilizing the talent and opportunities within the Human Resource Department.

1.10 Importance of Strategic Human Resource Management

When a human resource department strategically develops its plans for recruitment, training, and compensation based on the goals of the organization, it is ensuring a greater chance of organizational success.

Let's understand this concept in relation to a Cricket Team, where we assume that one player A is strategic HR department and all other players (B through H) assumed to be other departments. The entire team wants to win the game. All players may be very highly skilled, trained and qualified individually, but if they don't play as a team they may not win the game. One great player doesn't always help the team to win the game. By our own experience of watching so many Cricket matches, we understand that 11 great players cannot win the match if all of them focus only on their Batting performance. A team wins when its members support each other and work together for a common purpose. The same phenomenon is applicable to organization also. Individual departments may be very good, highly skilled and competent, but if they do not support and complement each other the organization may not sustain. For organization to become successful and remain competitive, the departments must complement each other and help overcome them their weaknesses. The player A (Strategic HR department) must co-ordinate with B, C, D. etc. (other departments). They must play as per their plan which they had thought of beforehand, support when required to help another player to remain on striking position to hit boundaries, and compensate the weakness of one player in order to bring a strong team as a whole.

When team works together to reach its goal then there are higher chances of achieving success. We can correlate Strategic HRM as the team captain or coach as his/ her responsibilities are somewhat different than other departments. Strategic HR departments are responsible for analyzing the weaknesses of various departments and providing the department with the necessary resources to overcome those weaknesses.

Concerns of Strategic Human Resource Management:
1. Assessing external environment for opportunities and threats
2. Preparing SWOT analysis of the organization, so as to match strengths and weaknesses of the organization with the external threats and opportunities.
3. Implementation of planned strategies.
4. Evaluation of strategies after their implementation to understand the effectiveness of the strategies and if required to make necessary changes in the strategies.

1.11 Nature of Strategic Human Resource Management

1. **To develop Competence:** SHRM makes sure that organization has highly motivated, competent employees which are required for sustainable competitive advantage.
2. **Direction:** It gives direction to the organization by aligning objectives of individual employees and all other departments with those of organization.
3. **Integration:** It integrates all the departments of the organization by setting a unified framework which is synergistically aligned with organizations vision.
4. **Enhancing the benefits:** SHRM provides a means through which organization uses the competence of its human resource for enhancing the benefits.

1.12 Models of Human Resource Management

Generally there are 4 models of Strategic Human Resource Management. Their purpose is as follows:

- They provide an analytical framework for studying Human resource management (for example, situational factors, stakeholders, strategic choice levels, competence)

- They legitimize certain HRM practices; a key issue here being the distinctiveness of HRM practices: "It is not the presence of selection or training but a distinctive approach to selection or training that matters".
- They provide a characterization of human resource management that establishes variables and relationship to be researched.
- They serve as a heuristic device-something to help us discover and understand the world for explaining the nature and significance of key HR practices.

Following are the Four HRM models:

1. The Fombrun, 2. The Harvard, 3. The Guest, and 4. The Warwick.

1. The Fombrun Model/ Matching Model:

Fombrun et al (1984)[1] proposed the 'matching model', which indicated that HR systems and the organization structure should be managed in a way that is congruent with organizational strategy. This point was made in their classic statement that: 'The critical management task is to align the formal structure and human resource systems so that they drive the strategic objectives of the organization'. Thus they took the first steps towards the concept of strategic HRM.This is the first HRM model. This model emphasises on four functions of HRM and their inter-relatedness. These four functions are: Selection, Appraisal, Development and Rewards. The model proposed that these four functions of HRM are anticipated to contribute to organizational effectiveness.

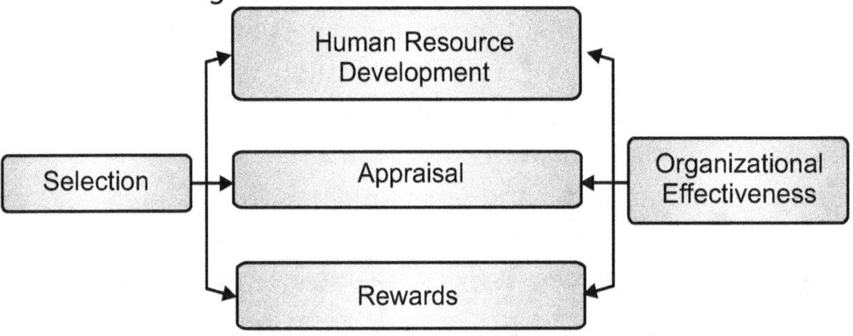

Fig. 1.3: Fombrun Model

The Fombrun Model is incomplete as it focuses on only four functions and does not count environmental and other contingency factors that affect HRM.

2. The Harvard Model of HRM

Beer et al (1984)[2] produced what has become known as the 'Harvard framework'. They started with the proposition that: 'Human Resource Management (HRM) involves all management decisions and actions that affect the nature of the relationship between the organization and employees – its human resources. 'They believed that: 'Today... many pressures are demanding a broader, more comprehensive and more strategic perspective

---

[1]Fombrun, C. J., Tichy, N. M., and Devanna, M. A. (1984). *Strategic Human resource management*. Wiley.
[2]Beer, M., Spector, B. A., Lawrence, P. R., Mills, D. Q., and Walton, R. E. (1984). *Managing human assets*. Simon and Schuster.

with regard to the organization's human resources' (ibid: 4). They also stressed that it was necessary to adopt 'a longer-term perspective in managing people and consideration of people as a potential asset rather than merely a variable cost'. Beer and his colleagues were the first to underline the HRM tenet that it belongs to line managers. They suggested that HRM had two characteristic features: (a) line managers accept more responsibility for ensuring the alignment of competitive strategy and HR policies; (b) HR has the mission of setting policies that govern how HR activities are developed and implemented in ways that make them more mutually reinforcing.

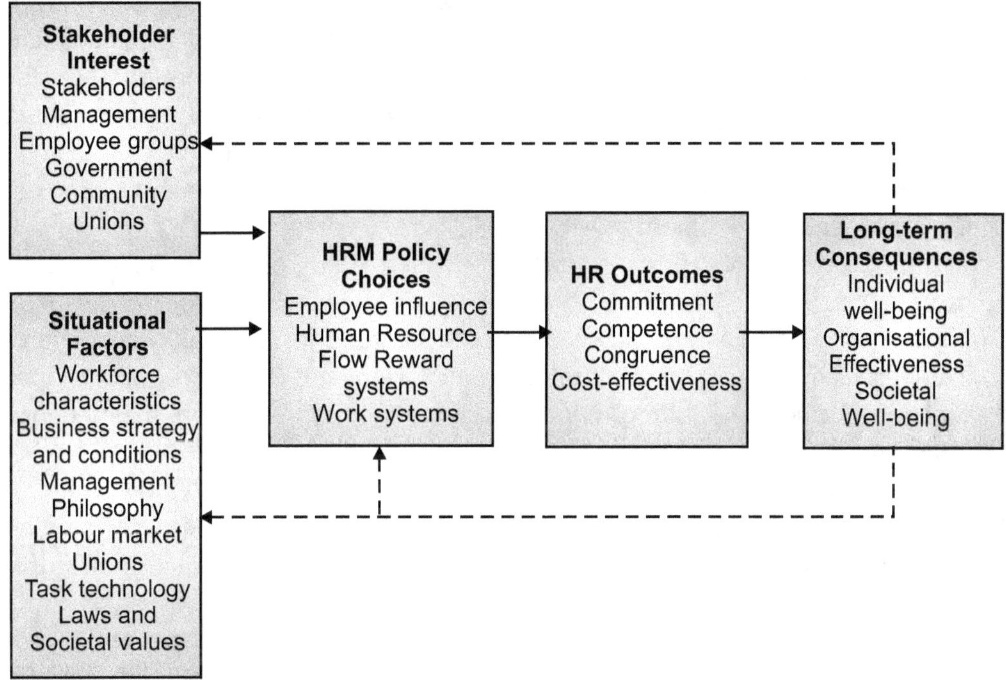

Fig. 1.4: Harvard Model of HRM

3. The Guest Model:

This model was developed by David Guest in 1997. This model emphasizes on the assumption that HR managers has specific strategies to begin with, which demand certain practices and when executed will result in outcomes.

4. The Warwick Model:

This model was developed by two researchers, Hendry and Pettigrew of University of Warwick. The model centres around five elements:

(a)   Outer context (Macro environmental forces).

(b)   Inner context (Micro environmental forces).

(c)   Business strategy content.

(d)   HRM context.

(e)   HRM content.

Points to Remember

1. Human Resources refer to the Knowledge, Skills, Education, Training and Proficiency of the members of the organization.
2. The Primary objective of HRM is to take care of the work life of employees even while ensuring their best possible co-operation for achieving the organizational goals and objectives.
3. The Scope of HRM is very wide which consists of acquisition, development, maintenance/retention, and control of human resources in the organization.
4. The Features of HRM includes Universal Force, Decision oriented, Focus on individual needs and objectives, Employee oriented, Employees- An Internal Customers, Development and growth oriented, Strategic implications, Support functions, Multidisciplinary nature, and ongoing and forward looking nature.
5. The Role of HRM includes- Conscience role, Counselor, Mediator, Spokesman, Change agent, and Problem solver.
6. The importance of HRM is further divided into organizational, social and professional.
7. The Function of HRM are classified into two categories such as Managerial which includes: Planning, Organizing, Staffing, Controlling, and Directing while its operative functions includes Recruiting/hiring, development, compensation, maintenance and integration.
8. Challenges of HRM includes – Environmental, Organizational, and Individual.
9. Strategic Human Resource Management (SHRM) is a process of aligning HR strategies with business strategies to accomplish performance goals through employee competency and commitment.
10. Importance of SHRM are: (i) It is accomplished at the top management level; (ii) It focuses on the expansion of process capabilities; (iii) It is inter-related with business strategies; (iv) Strategy formulation tasks rest with the line managers; and (v) Employees are viewed as strategic capabilities of the firm.
11. There are various models of SHRM such as The Fombrun/ The Matching Model; The Harvard, The Guest, and The Warwick.

Skill Development Exercise for Students

1. **Objective:** It is how to design and apply modern HR concepts more effectively in a specific situation to improve employee satisfaction, co-operation and performance.
2. **Procedure Note:** The class is divided into groups. Each group has (1) An HR Manager, (2) 2 HR Team Members, (3) 2 Representatives, and (4) 2 Observers of the meetings. The role of the observer is to observe and report on various aspects of the role playing sessions.

3. **Situation:** Tarun joins as a HR Manager of Spike Tyres and Tubes Limited. When he interacts with the employees of the company as a part of the familiarization process, he finds out to his shock that most of the employees have one grievance against the organization or another. His subordinates in the department also inform him that the employees are never satisfied with the benefits offered to them. Particularly when some benefits are given to one group of employees, while the other become agitated and demands benefits. For instance when some perks are provided to Younger employees, the older ones gets upset. Sometimes, the situation turns the round way also. Further the women employees who have joined the company in large numbers in recent years have a complain that the company has no women specific welfare measures like child care center and maternity benefits. However when Tarun scrutinizes the HR policies of the company, he realizes that the HR policies are the major source of troubles as they are old fashioned and do not suit the diversified and well informed workforce of today. This, he decides to conduct the meetings to discuss the alterations and improvement required to be made in HR policies and procedures in tune with the changing nature of the workforce.

4. **Steps in the Exercise**- There are 3 steps in the exercise:
    (a) The HR Manager meets the Representatives to take their views on the proposed changes to the existing HR policies.
    (b) HR manager convenes a meeting attended by 2 HR team members to finalize the changes to be incorporated in the HR policies. The updated HR policy will be subsequently be sent to the top management for further approval.
    (c) Observers will have to analyze and provide feedback on the performance of the members in the role playing session.

Questions for Discussion

1. What is HRM? Explain its objectives, scope and features in detail.
2. "HRM is the basic responsibility of every manager"- Elucidate.
3. "HRM functions plays an important role in the whole scheme of management of an industrial organization"- Discuss.
4. Explain in detail the Role of HRM.
5. Discuss the importance of HRM in the contemporary business environment.
6. What is Strategic HRM? Explain the nature of it.
7. If you were Human Resource Manager, then how will you introduce Strategic HRM?
8. Explain the models of Strategic HRM in detail with diagram.

Case Study

Strategic Human Resource Management in Wal-Mart Stores

Sam Walton established Wal-Mart Store in 1962 on three revolutionary philosophies; respect for the individual, service to our customers and strive for excellence. Walmart, Inc. is not only the largest discounted retailer in the world, it now also ranks as the largest corporation in the world. The retail giant dwarfs its nearest competition, generating three times the revenues of the world's number two retailer, France's Carrefour SA. Domestically, Wal-Mart has more than 1.2 million workers, making it the nation's largest nongovernmental employer. U.S. operations include 1,478 Wal-Mart discount stores (located in all 50 states.

Its international operations commenced in 1991 covering Canada and Puerto Rico; Wal-Mart Supercenters in Argentina, Brazil, China, Germany, Mexico, Puerto Rico, South Korea, and the United Kingdom (http://www.referenceforbusiness.com/history2/20/Wal-Mart-Stores-Inc.html#ixzz56lss8VII).

Walmart Company strives to maintain its competitive advantage through its satellite-based distribution system, and by keeping store location costs to a minimum by placing stores on low-cost land outside small to medium-sized towns, no matter in the US or in its abroad affiliations

Corporate strategy and HR strategy at Wal-Mart

Walmart purchased massive quantities of items from its suppliers to form scale economy, and with the efficient stock control system, help in making its operating costs lower than those of its competitors. It also imported many goods from China, "the world factory" for its low cost.

Managers engage in three levels of strategic planning (Gary Dessler, 2005): the corporate-level strategy; the business-level strategy and the function-level strategy. The functional strategy should serve the overall company strategy, so the corporate strategy could be implemented more effectively and efficiently.

The basic premise that underlying SHRM is that organizations adopting a particular strategy require HR practices that are different from those required by organizations adopting alternative strategies (Jackson and Schuler, 1995). Generally, there are two primary SHRM theoretical models the universalistic best practices and the contingency perspective of "best fit". The contingency perspective of "best fit elucidates that the individual HR practices will be selected based on the contingency of the specific context of a company. As

Wal-Mart has different corporate strategy with those retailers with differentiation strategy, which actually cultivates the primary contingency factor in the SHRM literature. What's more, we should be reminded that the individual HR practices will interact with firm strategy to result in organizational performance, and this interaction effects make the "universal best practices" may not apply so well in a specific company.

The following part we'll examine the "fitness" of HR practices in Walmart with this theoretical model, which is obviously also the integration process of HR practices with the contingency variables to some extent. From the recruitment, for example, the New York Times (January 2004) reported on an internal Wal-Mart audit which found "extensive violations of child-labour laws and state regulations requiring time for breaks and meals." The cheap price of children labours and minors make it earn more cost competitive advantage over other companies. Wal-Mart also faced a barrage of lawsuits alleging that the company discriminates against workers with disabilities, for the recruitment of these people means providing more facilities for them and the loss of efficiency to some extent.

From training perspective, through training on behavioural requirement for success and encouragement, Wal-mart tried to adjust the employee behaviours and competencies to what the company's strategy requires, that is to low down cost more. This logic is also embodied in its "lock-in" of its night-time shift in various stores. Through this enforced policy, Wal-mart tried to prevent "shrinkage" behaviour of its employees, to eliminate unauthorized cigarette breaks or quick trips home.

From the performance management perspective, Wal-mart made very high demanding standards and job designs. The New York Times reported Wal-mart had extensive violations of state regulations requiring time for breaks and meals. There are so many instances of minors working too late, during school hours, or for too many hours in a day, for the performance appraising just force them to do so. In the Career management, Walmart also goes great lengths to reduce cost, there are many cases that women sued Walmart for its discriminated policy against women by systematically denying them promotions and paying them less than men did. Women are pushed into "female" departments and are demoted if they complain about unequal treatment just for more cost reduction against its competitors.

From the compensation management perspective, Walmart has also showed very aggressive HR policies and activities. Walmart imported $15 billion worth of goods from china, for not only the strategic consideration of supplier chain economy, but also Walmart has some factories in china, whose products are branded with Walmart name. With this method, Walmart pays much less to Chinese labours in this "world-factory" and earn some advantages, so we could just see how the Walmart corporate strategy is just intensely integrated with its HR policy. In 2002, operating costs for Walmart were just 16.6 percent of total sales, compared to a 20.7 average for the retail industry as a whole, which supported greatly the overall strategy. Walmart workers in California earn on average 31 percent less than workers employed in other large retail business. Actually, with other operating and inventory costs set by higher-level management, store managers must turn to wages to increase profits, and Walmart expects the labour costs to be cut by two-tenths of a percentage point each year.

From the employee benefit and safety perspective, workers eligible for benefits such as health insurance must pay over the odds for them. In 1999, employees paid 36 percent of the costs. In 2001, the employee burden rose to 42 percent. While in the US, large-firm employees pay on average 16 percent of the premium for health insurance. Unionized supermarket workers typically pay nothing. Walmart was frequently accused of not providing employees with affordable access to health care, but the top managers and HR managers know their focus was just to try their most to implement Walmart's corporate strategy.

Finally, from the labour relations perspective, Sam Walton sought to bring great value through aggressive discounting to customers. Because unionized supermarket workers typically pay nothing, Walmart has strong anti-union policy. Allegations of firing workers sympathetic to labour organizations have been made, all new employees are shown a propaganda video tape, which said joining a union, would have bad implication for them, and the employees should never sign a union card. In the UK it was reported in the Guardian that Walmart is facing the prospect of a bruising legal battle with the GMB trade union in a row over collective bargaining rights, for the union would not accepting Walmart withdrew a 10% pay offer to more than 700 workers after they rejected a new package of terms and conditions, which included giving up rights to collective pay bargaining. Here there may be some doubt why Walmart has recently allowed unionization in their stores in China, where unionization is mandatory. But actually, this mandatory rule is made a long time before Walmart walk into china, so why Walmart give up its persistence in not having some unions, and its former reason to China government is that it did not have any unions in its global working. So how do we see Walmart's compromise if that constitutes a "compromise"?

It has been argued that doing business in China is particularly difficult because of the higher relative importance of personal relationships (guanxi), as opposed to the specification and enforcement of contracts in the West (Davies et al, 1995). Walmart China has tried every effort to develop good relationships with China government and other influence groups. So, Walmart made this exception of have unionizations is just in accordance with its corporate strategy and HR strategy. If it ignores the Chinese government's firm rule, its cost would just outweigh what it would save by organizing no unions in its labor relations management as Walmart provides little power for Chinese workers as the unions are controlled by the state.

Conclusion:

Therefore, from all those above content we know the human resource management is of strategic importance to Walmart. Both the top managers and HR executives should pay more attention to the everyday employment management. They should play more roles that are positive in training and using their human resources, and may be cultivating better organization culture, all of which may prove more cost saving, and correspondingly help realize Sam Walton's simple philosophy of "bringing more value to customers".

Based on the case answer these two questions:

1. Identify the challenges your business will face and how it will affect your HRM strategies.

2. Design HRM strategies to address these business challenge.

Questions from Previous MBA Examinations

1. Discuss the importance of Human Resource management.   **(April 2006)**

Ans. Refer Article 1.7 of this chapter.

2. What is Human Resource Management.   **(April 2006)**

Ans. Refer Articles 1.1 and 1.2 of this chapter.

3. Define Human Resource Management.   **(April 2009, 2010)**

Ans. Refer Article 1.2 of this chapter.

4. Define Human Resource Management and elaborate its importance and also discuss its evolution.   **(December 2009)**

Ans. Refer Articles 1.2, 1,1 and 1.3 of this chapter.

5. Explain the Nature, Objectives and Scope of HRM.   **(December 2010)**

Ans. Refer Articles 1.5, 1.3 and 1.4 of this chapter.

6. Define HRM. Explain the various Functions of HRM.   **(April 2011)**

Ans. Refer Articles 1.2 and 1.8 of this chapter.

7. Explain the concept of HRM. **(April 2012)**

Ans. Refer Articles 1.1 and 1.2 of this chapter.

8. Discuss the importance of HRM and explain HRM functions and objectives with examples. **(April 2016)**

Ans. Refer Articles 1.7, 1.8 and 1.5 of this chapter.

9. What are various models of HRM ? Explain atleast one model in detail. **(April 2016)**

Ans. Refer Article 1.12 of this chapter.

10. Explain the Importance of HRM. **(April 2017)**

Ans. Refer Article 1.7 of this chapter.

11. Define HRM. **(April 2018)**

Ans. Refer Article 1.2 of this chapter.

12. Explain the Scope and Functions of HRM. **(April 2018)**

Ans. Refer Articles 1.4 and 1.8 of this chapter.

13. Define HRM and explain various functions of HRM. **(April 2015)**

Ans. Refer Articles 1.2 and 1.8 of this chapter.

14. Explain the Nature and Scope of HRM. **(December 2017)**

Ans. Refer Articles 1.5 and 1.4 of this chapter.

References

I. https://www.scribd.com/document/325920873/HRM-Case-Study-With-Solutions

II. https://www.chegg.com/homework-help/questions-and-answers/case-study-strategic-human-resource-management-wal-mart-stores-introduction-sam-walton-est-q27112359

HR Acquisition and Retention

Contents ...

Learning Objectives:

- ➢ Understand the significance and importance of Human Resource Planning
- ➢ Know the process and challenges of Human Resource Planning
- ➢ Differentiate between Job description and Job specification
- ➢ Identify the factors affecting Job Design
- ➢ Differentiate between Job enrichment and Job enlargement
- ➢ Understand the process of recruitment and selection
- ➢ Understand the importance of retention of employees

Opening Vignette/Pragmatic Insight: The McDonald concept was introduced in San Bernardino, California by Dick and Mac McDonald of Manchester, New Hampshire. It was modified and expanded by their business partner, Ray Kroc of Oak Park, Illinois who later brought out the business interests of the McDonald brothers in the concept and went to found McDonald's Corporation. McDonald's is the world's leading fast food company by sales of 32,000 restaurants serving burgers and fries in about 120 countries serving 47 million customers each day.

There are nearly 14000 golden Arches locations in the US. Most of its outlets are free standing units, but McDonald's has many units located in airports and retail areas. Moreover, McDonalds is one of the world most well-known and valuable brands and increasing share in the globally. Today more than 2.6 million people trust McDonalds and go to eat due to provide good food with a high standard, quick service and value of money.

To achieve the McDonald's goals, human resource planning is concerned with getting the right people, using them perfectly, and training and developing them. In order to meet McDonald's aims and objectives successfully, people are rightly identified and are train to spot out any problem that are likely to occur. They should be capable to providing the best solution during such times. Like all other businesses, McDonald's also need assistance of its staff members to carry out is daily activities. All the staff members fulfill its key role in its operation of business. If the manager of the McDonald's do not select the potential employees in a careful way, then it can create number of problems such as, poor productivity levels, no good feeling among the staff members, job dissatisfaction, high absenteeism, customer complaints, dismissal, replacement etc. For demand of labour, McDonald's analysis its future plans and estimate the levels of activity within McDonald's. As a result, they can predict that the organization has right number of potential employee with right quality.

The external labour market is very important for any organisation because of it can make up of potential employees, locally, regionally, who have the right skills and qualification necessary at any time. For McDonald's, local unemployment figures are very important who give the indication of the general labour availability required at that time. Also, Human resource planning of McDonald's includes searching at how labour is organised within a business or an organisation.

Thus the HR planning process at McDonald's and its accomplishments clearly establish the relevance of good HR plans behind its success. Let us now discuss in depth with the help of this chapter.

Adapted from: https://www.essay.uk.com/free-essays/business/human-resource-management-planning-and-development.php

HR Acquisition- A Conceptual Framework

Recruitment and selection of workforce/ manpower is termed as HR acquisition. The term HR acquisition is used for the process of hiring people keeping long term perspective in mind.

Human Resource Planning

2.1 Introduction to Human Resource Planning

Human Resource Planning is basically the business process for ensuring that an organization has suitable access to talents and also to ensure future business success. It is basically the process of identifying the right person for the right job at the right time and at the right cost. It is also called as "Manpower Planning or Manpower Management. The success of any organization depends largely on the quality and quantity of the workforce. Before selecting the right man for the right job, it becomes necessary for any organization to determine the quality and quantity of the workforce. This is basically the main function of Human Resource Planning.

Human Resource Planning deals with staff requirement, looking after present and future demands for various skills and the availability of the individuals with those skills. It is the process by which the organisation determines how a management should move from its current manpower position to the desired manpower position. The three basic objectives of any Human Resource Planning are:

- Attracting, Developing and retaining an efficient workforce.
- Evaluating and Rewarding its performance.
- Inventing and controlling HR plans and Programmes to optimize the HR cost.

However the direct purpose of Human Resource Planning is to investigate, forecast, plan, control and match the demand for and supply of manpower. The main task of Human Resource Planning is to scan the environment in order to identify the availability of people with appropriate skills and characteristics. In the past the term Human Resource Planning was considered as a short term activity and a problem of the line managers. However due to technological advancement and other changes in the environment organizations are forced to view Human Resource Planning as its both short and long term activities.

The essence of Human Resource Planning is the identification of the demand and supply of the labour to accomplish the organizational goals on a sustained basis.

2.2 Definitions of Human Resource Planning

HR planning is a process that identifies current and future human resources needs for an organization to achieve its goals. Human resource planning should serve as a link between human resource management and the overall strategic plan of an organization.

Bulla and Scott defined HR planning as-*"the process for ensuring that the human resource requirements of an organization are identified and plans are made for satisfying those requirements".*

Reilly defines HR planning as *"A process in which an organization attempts to estimate the demand for labour and evaluate the size, nature and sources of supply which will be required to meet the demand."*

2.3 Objectives of Human Resource Planning

1. **Achieve Goal:** Human Resource Planning helps in achieving individual, Organizational and National goals. Since Human resource planning is linked with career planning, it can able to achieve individual goal while achieving organisational and national goals.

2. **Estimates Future Organizational Structure and Manpower Requirements:** Human Resource Planning is related with number of personnel required for the future, job-family, age distribution of employees, qualification and desired experience, salary range etc and thereby determines future organisation structure.

3. **Human Resource Audit:** Human resource planning process is comprised of estimating the future needs and determining the present supply of Manpower Resources. Manpower supply analysis is done through skills inventory. This helps in preventing over staffing as well as under-staffing.

4. **Job Analysis:** The process of studying and collecting information relating to operations and responsibilities of a specific job is called Job analysis. Job analysis is comprised of job description and job specification. Job description describes the duties and responsibilities of a particular job in an organized factual way. Job specification specifies minimum acceptable human qualities necessary to perform a particular job properly.

2.4 Need for Human Resource Planning

An organisation must plan out its human resource requirements well in advance so that it could compete effectively with its competitors in the market. A well thought-out-human resource plan provides adequate lead time for recruitment, selection and training of personnel. It becomes all the more crucial because the lead time for procuring personnel is a time consuming process and in certain cases one may not always get the requisite type of personnel needed for the jobs. Non-availability of suitable manpower may result in postponement or delays in executing new projects and expansion programmes which ultimately lead to lower efficiency and productivity further. To be specific, the following are the needs for human resource planning:

1. **Shortage of Skills:** These days we find shortage of skills in people. So it is necessary to plan for such skilled people much in advance than when we actually need them. Non-availability of skilled people when and where they are needed is an important factor which prompts sound Human Resource Planning. Human Resource Planning is essential because of frequent labour turnover which is unavoidable by all means. Labour turnover arises because of discharges, marriages, promotion, transfer etc which causes a constant ebb and flow in the workforce in the organisation.

2. **Changing Needs of Technology:** Due to changes in technology and new techniques of production, existing employees need to be trained or new blood injected into an organisation. Manpower planning is needed in order to identify

areas with a surplus of personnel or areas in which there is a shortage of personnel. If there is a surplus, it can be re-deployed, or if there is a shortage new employees can be procured.

3. **Changes in Organisation Design and Structure:** Due to changes in organisation structure and design, we need to plan the required human resources right from the beginning.

2.5 Importance of Human Resource Planning

The failure in planning and in developing personnel will prove to be a limiting factor in attributing to the organizational objectives. If the number of persons in an organization is less than the number of persons required to carry out the organizational plans, there will be disruptions in the flow of work and the production will also be lowered. But if, on the other hand, some persons are surplus in an organization, they will have to be paid remuneration. The sound personnel policy requires that there should be adequate number of persons of the right type to attain its objectifies.

For this the manpower planner should be concerned with the training and the scheduling of the planning of personnel and persuading the management to use the results of manpower planning studies in the conduct of the business. Every industrial or commercial organization has the need of proper system of manpower planning so as to bring efficiency and economy in the organization. Smaller concerns and those with simpler organizations also require human resource planning though on a small scale. Human resource planning can prove to be an important aid to frame the training and development programmes for the personnel because it takes into account the effects of anticipated changes in technology, markets and products on manpower requirements and educational and training programme requirements.

Human resource planning is relatively a difficult task for the personnel management. It is particularly so in business enterprises which are often subject to forces outside their control such as social, political and economic changes. Manpower is a key resource required for the achievement of business objectives. Materials, equipments, power and other resources can be effectively and efficiently used, only if there is manpower capable of processing them into required goods and services. It takes a long time to develop the manpower of right type to use these resources. Therefore, decisions concerning manpower development must be taken many years in advance. However, management may stick to short periods for rank and file employees, but it will have to concentrate upon the problems of replacing key professional and managerial personnel on a long term basis. In as-much-as many big organizations do prepare long-range forecasts in production, marketing and capital investment; it should not be surprising if it makes long term projections in regard to its personnel. However, human resource plans cannot be rigid or static, they can be modified or adjusted according to the change in the circumstances.

2.6 Process of Human Resource Planning

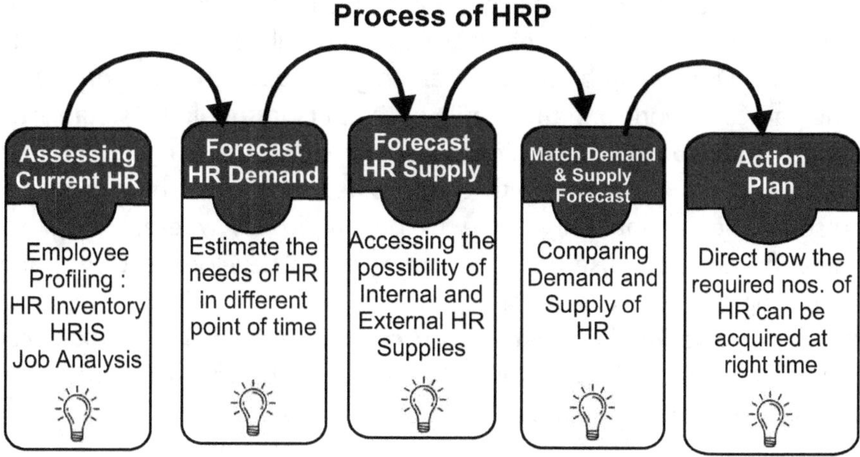

Fig. 2.1: Process of HR Planning

For planning Human resource requirements it is essential that the organization has set its goals. Based on the strategic goals of the organization; Human Resource planning is conducted through six steps as explained here.

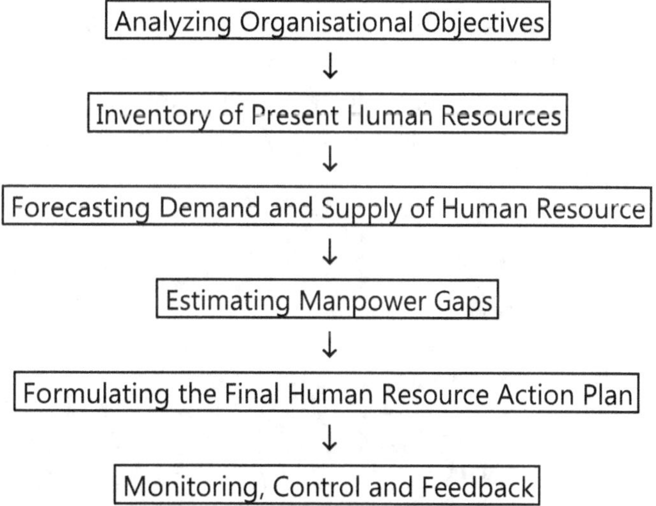

1. **Analysing Organizational Objectives:** The objective to be achieved in future in various fields such as production, marketing, finance, expansion and sales gives the idea about the work to be done in the organization.

2. **Inventory of Present Human Resources:** From the updated human resource information storage system, the current number of employees, their capacity, performance and potential can be analysed. To fill the various job requirements, the internal sources (i.e., employees from within the organization) and external sources (i.e., candidates from various placement agencies) can be estimated.

3. **Forecasting Demand and Supply of Human Resource:** The human resources required at different positions according to their job profile are to be estimated. The available internal and external sources to fulfill those requirements are also measured. There should be proper matching of job description and job specification of one particular work, and the profile of the person should be suitable to it.

4. **Estimating Manpower Gaps:** Comparison of human resource demand and human resource supply will provide with the surplus or deficit of human resource. Deficit represents the number of people to be employed, whereas surplus represents termination. Extensive use of proper training and development programme can be done to upgrade the skills of employees.

5. **Formulating the Final Human Resource Action Plan:** The human resource plan depends on whether there is deficit or surplus in the organization. Accordingly, the plan may be finalized either for new recruitment, training, interdepartmental transfer in case of deficit of termination, or voluntary retirement schemes and redeployment in case of surplus.

6. **Monitoring, Control and Feedback:** It mainly involves implementation of the human resource action plan. Human resources are allocated according to the requirements, and inventories are updated over a period. The plan is monitored strictly to identify the deficiencies and remove it. Comparison between the human resource plan and its actual implementation is done to ensure the appropriate action and the availability of the required number of employees for various jobs.

1. **Mayo Clinic**

Source: Human Resources, MBA

Consistently ranked as one of Fortune's 100 Best Companies to Work For, Mayo Clinic has built a reputation as a place for employing the brightest minds to offer the most passionate service. The key to the company's success is the team dynamic promoted by the human resource department at Mayo Clinic. According to HR personnel, there are 60,000 employees who link arms with one another to provide support and care for Mayo Clinic's patients and families. How does Mayo Clinic provide such a team-focused dynamic in the workplace? Management credibility, internal communication, and extensive on-the-job training. Employees feel prepared to handle situations and receive recognition for their efforts.

2. Ford

Source: Human Resources, MBA

Ford is the car manufacturer that broke ideals when it came to hiring practices and leadership. Henry Ford is recognized as one of the best leaders the world has ever seen. His philosophies and beliefs trickled into the HR department at Ford. Today the company is recognized for its HR innovation through a highly disciplined culture, outstanding training opportunities, and strong and consistent processes. When it comes to human resource practice, the company focuses on implementing healthy communication through the removal of emotion and reliance on data. HR believes data and discipline should come first, before emotion. When the process is adhered to, a healthy work environment succeeds. Ford has consistently been named a leader in HR practice by People Management.

2.7 Guidelines for making Human Resource Planning Effective

1. **Adequate Information System:** The main problem faced in Human Resource Planning is the lack of information. So an adequate Human resource database should be maintained/developed for better coordinated and more accurate Human Resource Planning.

2. **Participation:** To be successful, Human Resource Planning requires active participation and coordinated efforts on the part of operating executives. Such participation will help to improve understanding of the process and thereby, reduce resistance from the top management.

3. **Adequate Organisation:** Human Resource Planning should be properly organised. A separate section or committee may be constituted within the human resource department to provide adequate focus and to coordinate the planning efforts at various levels.

4. **Human Resource Planning should be Balanced with Corporate Planning:** Human resource plans should be balanced with the corporate plans of the enterprise. The methods and techniques used should fit the objectives, strategies and environment of the particular organisation.

5. **Appropriate Time Horizon:** The period of manpower plans should be appropriate according to the needs and circumstances of the specific enterprise. The size and structure of the enterprise as well as the changing aspirations of the people should be taken into consideration.

2.8 Barriers to Human Resource Planning

1. **Resistance by Employers:** Many employers resist Human Resource Planning as they think that it increases the cost of manpower for the management. Further, employers feel that Human Resource Planning is not necessary as candidates will be available as and when required in the country due to the growing unemployment situation.

2. **Resistance by Employees:** Employees resist Human Resource Planning as it increases the workload on the employees and prepares programmes for securing human resources mostly from outside.

3. **Inadequacies in Quality of Information:** Reliable information about the economy, other industries, Labour markets, trends in human resources etc are not easily available. This leads to problems while planning for human resources in the organisation.

4. **Uncertainties:** Uncertainties are quite common in human resource practices in India due to absenteeism, seasonal unemployment, labour turnover etc. Further, the uncertainties in the industrial scenario like technological changes and marketing conditions also cause imperfection in Human Resource Planning. It is the uncertainties that make Human Resource Planning less reliable.

5. **Time and Expense:** Human Resource Planning is a time-consuming and expensive exercise. A good deal of time and cost are involved in data collection and forecasting.

Google's HRM: HR Planning

Source: http://panmore.com/google-hrm-hr-planning-job-analysis-design

Google HRM human resource management, HR planning, job analysis, design, description, specification, forecasting, HR supply, demand.

Google's Offices in New York City

Google's human resource management effectively addresses concerns on human resource planning, job analysis, and job design. (Photo: Public Domain)

Google's human resource management involves different strategies to address the workforce needs of this diversified business organization. This diversification imposes significant challenges to human resource managers of the company. Nonetheless, there are certain HRM approaches that are generally applied to different areas of Google. For instance, in human resource planning, Google's HR managers focus on the effective use of forecast information to minimize the surplus or shortage of employees, and to establish a balance between the supply and demand for qualified employees. Google's job analysis and design approaches are also varied because of the different types of jobs in the different businesses of the company.

Google's Human Resource Planning

Forecasting: Human resource managers at Google use trend analysis and scenario analysis for forecasting. Trend analysis is a quantitative technique that allows the company to predict possible HR demand based on current conditions and changes in the business. Scenario analysis is Google's qualitative technique for forecasting HR demand. Scenario analysis involves analyzing different combinations of variables to predict HR demand for each resulting scenario. In this way, Google uses a combination of quantitative and qualitative techniques for forecasting HR demand.

Surplus and Shortage of Employees: Concerns about surplus or shortage of employees at Google are mostly in the production processes, such as the manufacture of Chromecast and the provision of the Google Fiber Internet and cable television service. In developing and providing web-based and software products, human resource surplus and shortage are not a significant concern. For production processes, Google's human resource management identifies possible surpluses and shortages through forecasting techniques. Thus, the company's human resource planning includes forecasted surpluses and shortages of human resources. Such information is used for recruitment and scheduling.

Balancing Supply and Demand: Google's human resource management faces minimal problems when it comes to balancing HR supply and demand. Even if demand for web-based/software products and online advertising services increase, Google does not need to commensurately increase its human resources in these business areas because of the digital nature of these products. Still, the company needs to address HR supply and demand in other areas, such as the production and distribution of consumer electronics like Nexus and Chromecast. For these areas, Google uses a flexible strategy where new employees are hired based on forecasts of human resource needs.

The combination of Google's HR management approaches for forecasting, identifying issues with surplus and shortage of employees, and balancing of human resource supply and demand effectively supports the human resource needs of the firm. Google uses conventional methods and techniques together with advanced information systems to analyze human resource data to support human resource management decisions.

JOB ANALYSIS AT NESTLE

Nestlé is a global food, health and wellness company. The company was formed in 1905 when the Anglo-Swiss Milk Company and the Farine Lactée Henri Nestlé Company merged. The new company's first products were baby formula and condensed milk. The company has grown since that point and is now the largest company of its kind in the world. Its product line included bottled water, breakfast cereal, ice cream pet food, chocolate and baked goods. The company currently has offices in 191 countries worldwide and employee approximately 2, 83,000 people. Nestlé is looking for people who are creative, flexible and who consider the future to be an exciting place. The company values people who are interested in continuous learning while on the job. Good communication skills and the ability to motivate others is an important part of working for the company. Job analysis is the procedure for determining the duties and the skills requirements of the job and the kind of the person who should be hired for it. It is done by HR department of the Nestle Company. Nestle uses wide range of methods to figure out the relevant job analysis. It forms the basis which enables the prospective candidates to make an informal decision about their response to the job advertisements. Thus Job Analysis facilitates better management of Human Resources.

Adapted from: http://infofunnia.blogspot.com/2010/11/hrm-nestle.html

---

Job Analysis

2.9 Meaning of Job Analysis

Job analysis is a process of identifying and determining in detail the particular job duties and requirements and the importance of these duties for a given job. It helps an organization determine which employee is best for a specific job.

In other words, job analysis is used to determine placement of jobs. It allows human resource managers to identify the path of job progression for employers looking to advance their career and compensation.

To be clear, job analysis targets the job, not the person. Data for job analysis is collected from the job holders through interviews or questionnaires, but the result of analysis is a description of the job and not a description of the job holder.

2.10 Definitions of Job Analysis

Harry L. Wylie:

"Job analysis deals with the anatomy of the job.....This is the complete study of the job embodying every known and determinable factor, including the duties and responsibilities involved in its performance; the conditions under which performance is carried on; the nature of the task; the qualifications required in the worker; and the conditions of employment such as pay, hours, opportunities and privileges."

Michael J. Jucius:

"Job analysis refers to the process of studying the operations, duties and organisational aspects of jobs in order to derive specification, or as they are called by some job description".

2.11 Purpose of Job Analysis

Job analysis is used in preparation of job descriptions and job specifications which help in the hiring of right personnel for the job. The uses of Job analysis are as follows:

1. **Human Resource Planning:** HRP determines how many and what type of employees would be needed. To make HRP more effective, job related information is essential and thus job analysis is necessary for HRP.

2. **Recruitment and Selection:** For recruitment and selection Job Analysis is crucial because HR manager can recruit and select personnel of required skills and competencies only if Job analysis is available.

3. **Training and Development:** Job analysis helps HR managers to understand what a particular job demands from the employees. Job analysis also helps in the selection of trainees for particular training programme.

4. **Remuneration:** Job analysis helps determine wage and salary grades for jobs to be performed. Remuneration if based on the relative worth of each job can avoid perception of inequity among employees and thus can avoid demotivation.

5. **Performance Appraisal:** Performance appraisal assesses the actual performance of employees against the expected performance. Job analysis helps in deciding the target performance and therefore helps in deciding the promotion, transfer or training needs of employees.

6. **Health and Safety:** Job analysis may reveal the hazardous conditions and unhealthy environment factors such as excess heat, high level of noise, dust etc. Job analysis; therefore can provide an opportunity to implement corrective actions.

2.12 Process of Job Analysis

(Source:https://www.businesstopia.net/human-resource/job-analysis-definitions-methods-process-importance)

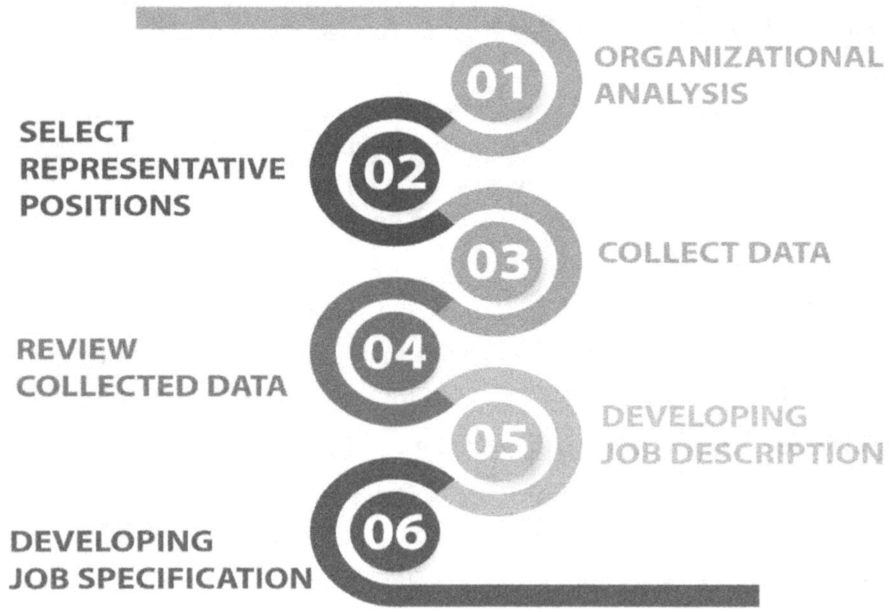

Fig. 2.2: Process of Job Analysis

Job analysis process involves the implementation of following steps:

1. **Organizational Analysis:** The first step in the job analysis process is to determine its purpose. This will help determine what kind of data to collect and how to collect it. The necessary background information for this step can be collected by using organization charts, process charts and job descriptions.

2. **Select Representative Positions:** It will be time consuming and costly to analyse all jobs in an organization. So, it is essential to select a representative sample of jobs for detail job analysis.

3. **Collect Data:** The next step is to collect job-related data such as educational qualification, duties, and responsibilities, working conditions, employee behaviour, skills and abilities. Data is collected by using methods such as observation, interviews and questionnaire.

4. **Review Collected Data:** A job analysis report is prepared by using the gathered data. The information is then verified with the worker performing the job and their supervisor.

5. **Developing Job Description:** The information collected is used to develop a written statement known as job description. Job description is a document that describes the responsibilities, working conditions, locations, risks and tasks required for effective job performance.

6. **Developing Job Specification:** The final step in the process is to develop job specification. Job specification and job descriptions are two tangible products of the job analysis process. Job specification is a statement of personal traits, educational qualification, experience, background and skills needed to perform a job.

Job Description Vs Job Specification:

The *critical difference* between job description and job specification is that; former is the summary of all the task, role and responsibilities specifying what the company is offering to the candidate; whereas, the latter is an overview of all the attributes, experience and qualification which the company is looking for in a candidate to pursue the job. Job description and job specification are the two essential components of job analysis.

Difference and Comparison between Job Description and Job Analysis:

Basis	Job description	Job specification
1. Meaning	Job description is the written document in which all the information regarding a particular job including role, responsibilities and duties is summarized in a systematic manner.	Job specification is the set of specific qualities, knowledge and experience, a person must possess to perform a particular job.
2. Origin	Originates from Job Analysis.	Based on Job Description.
3. Elements	Consist of job title, job location, role, responsibilities, duties, salary, incentives and allowances.	Involves personal attributes, skills, knowledge, educational qualification and experience.
4. Objective	Describes the job profile.	Specifies the eligibility criteria.
5. What is it?	What the company is offering to the candidate ?	What the company is demanding from the candidate ?
6. Application by Human Resource Manager	Used to give the sufficient and relevant information of the job.	Used to match the right attributes with the job so described.

Example: Let us assume that XYZ Ltd. is looking for a sales executive. It has posted the job description and job specification regarding the post, on a job portal. It looked something like this:

Job Description – Sales Executive

About Us: XYZ Ltd. is a well-renowned marketing and advertising company which has its branches spread all over the country with an approximately 500 employees working for it. The company is into B2B sales where its clients are usually big business firms and some of which are corporate leaders.

Job Title: Sales Executive

Role: We are looking for aspirant sales executives for the company. It is an office job where the candidate has to make outbound calls to convert prospective customers into clients. However, the candidate may need to travel to different cities at times. We are looking for someone who has excellent communication skills and convincing power.

Duties and Responsibilities:

1. Make outbound calls.
2. Create new clients.
3. Achieve sales targets.
4. Handle direct customer enquiries.
5. Prepare sales report.
6. Explore and grab new business opportunities.
7. Keep sales record on CRM software.

Job Specification – Sales Executive

Educational Qualification: Any graduate/MBA in Marketing or Sales is preferred. Good Personality, Skills and Competencies:

1. Excellent communication skills.
2. Positive attitude.
3. Ability to work under pressure.
4. Negotiation skills.
5. Customer handling ability.
6. Takes initiative and Capable of working for long hours.

Experience: 0-1 years of experience in a similar job profile is preferred.

(Adapted from: https://theinvestorsbook.com/job-description-vs-job-specification.html)

2.13 Components of Job Description

- *Job Title* is the name of the post vacant.
- *Job Location* is the branch of the company where the candidate will be posted after selection.
- *Role* refers to the arena of work and how the responsibilities are to be fulfilled, defined by the company.
- *Responsibilities and Duties* is a list of various job-related activities which the candidate is supposed to perform and take account of his actions.
- *Salary* is the pay scale which the company is ready to offer for that particular job. It may or may not be negotiable.
- *Incentives* refer to commission and remuneration associated with the targets achieved.

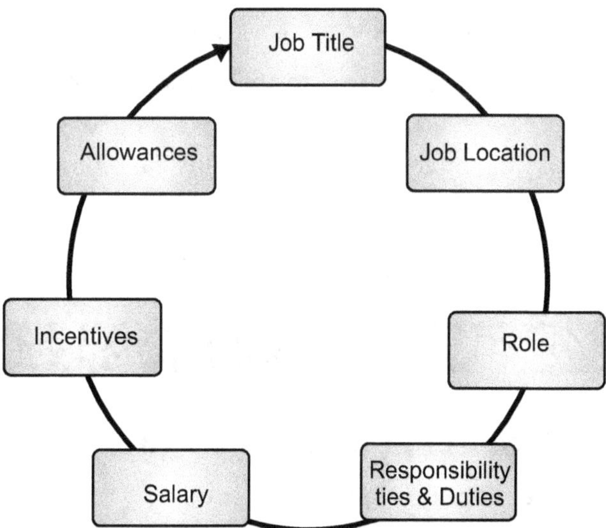

Fig. 2.3: Components of Job Description (Source: https://theinvestorsbook.com/job-description-vs-job-specification.html)

- *Allowances* are the other benefits and expenses which the company pays on behalf of the candidate.

2.14 Components of Job Specification

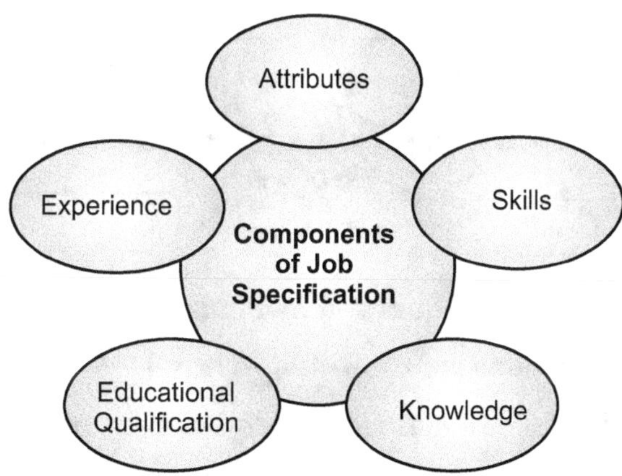

Fig. 2.4: Components of Job Specification

Source: https://theinvestorsbook.com/job-description-vs-job-specification.html

- *Educational Qualification* defines the specific requirement regarding academic knowledge of a person. It includes his school education, graduate, post-graduation and other such qualifications of which he holds degree or mark sheet.

- *Skills required* refers to the particular set of special abilities which are essential for the proper execution of the given tasks. The company may or may not ask for the certificate of training in such skills from the candidates.

- *Experience* is the information of all the past and present employment or association of the candidate, including the name of the company, post, duration, salary package, job profile, etc.

Job Design

2.15 Concept of Job Design

The **Job Design** means outlining the task, duties, responsibilities, methods and relationships required to perform the given set of a job. In other words, job design encompasses the components of the task and the interaction pattern among the employees, with the intent to satisfy both the organizational needs and the social needs of the jobholder.The objective of a job design is to arrange the work in such a manner so as to reduce the boredom and dissatisfaction among the employees, arising due to the repetitive nature of the task. There are several important methods and techniques that the management uses while designing the jobs. These are:

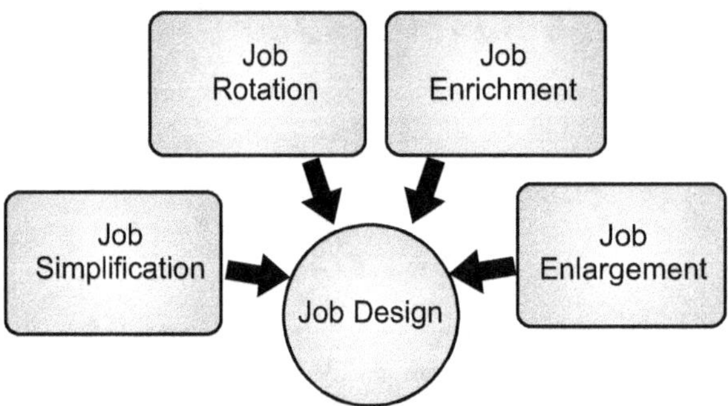

Fig. 2.5: Techniques and Methods of Job Design

(Source : https://businessjargons.com/job-design.html)

While designing the job, the following aspects are to be taken into the consideration:

1. The foremost requirement for a job design is to define clearly the task an individual is supposed to perform. A task is the piece of work assigned to the individual who has to perform it within the given time limits.

2. The management must decide on the level of motivation that is required to be enforced on an individual to get the work completed successfully. Thus, the managers must design the jobs that motivate his employees.

3. The managers must decide critically on the amount of resources that needs to be allocated to perform a particular type of a job. Thus, the efforts should be made to make an optimum utilization of organizational resources while designing the job so that the organization does not suffer any dilemma due to the shortage of its resources.

4. When the jobs are assigned to the individual, he agrees to do it because of the rewards attached to it. Thus, the manager must include in the job design the compensation, bonuses, incentives, benefits and other remuneration method for the employees.

Thus, the job should be designed with the intent to find a fit between the job and its performer, such that the job is performed efficiently, and the performer experiences satisfaction while performing it and give his best efforts towards its completion.

2.16 Factors affecting Job Design

Organizational, environmental and behavioural factors affect Job Design. A job which is properly designed will be productive and satisfying. If a job design is not appropriate, then it must be redesigned based on the feedback from employees. Various factors affecting Job Design are as follows:

1. Organizational Factors:

The various factors under organisational factors include task features, work flow, ergonomics, work practices, etc.

A brief description of these follows:

(a) **Task Features:** A job design involves a number of tasks performed by a group of workers. Further, each task consists of three internal features, namely, (i) planning, (ii) executing, and (iii) controlling. An ideal job design needs to integrate all these three features of tasks to be performed.

(b) **Work Flow:** The very nature of a product influences the sequences of jobs, i.e., work flow. In order to perform work in an effective and efficient manner, the tasks involved in a job need to be sequenced and balanced. Consider the car as a product. The frame of a car needs to be built before the fenders, and similarly the doors will be built later. Thus, once the sequences of tasks are determined, and then the balance between tasks is established.

(c) Ergonomics: Ergonomics refers to designing and shaping job in such a manner so as to strike a fit between the job and the job holder. In other words, jobs are designed in such a way to match job requirements with worker's physical abilities to perform a job effectively.

(d) Work Practices: Practice means a set way of doing work based on tradition or collective wishes of workers. While designing jobs, these work practices need to be taken into consideration. Evidences are available to state that ignoring work practices can result in undesirable consequences. F.W. Taylor determined work practices by time and motion study.

Such determination requires repeated observations. However, the accuracy of the determined work practice is subject to distortions depending on the competence of the observer and deviations from the normal work cycle. Another limitation of this method is its applicability only when production is underway.

2. Environmental Factors:

Environmental factors include social and cultural expectations, and employee ability and availability. These are discussed one by one as follows:

(a) Social and Cultural Expectations: Gone are days when workers were ready to do any job under any working conditions. But, with increase in their literacy, education, knowledge, awareness, etc. have raised their expectations from the jobs. In view of this, jobs for them need to be designed accordingly. It is due to this reason that the job design now is characterised by the features like work hours, rest breaks, vacations, religious beliefs, etc. Disregarding these social expectations can create dissatisfaction, low motivation, high turnover and low quality of working life.

(b) Employee Ability and Availability: The various task elements should be included in accordance with the employee abilities and capabilities. Incorporating job elements beyond the employee ability will be causing mismatch between the job and the job holder. Therefore, due consideration should be given to employee ability while determining job design. Henry Ford did follow it. He made job design simple and requiring little training for assembly line considering that most potential workers lacked any automobile-making experience.

3. Behavioural Factors:

Behavioural factors are based on the premise that people are influenced to work to satisfy their needs. Higher the need, more one finds job challenging. One's behaviour at work is governed by certain factors are:

(a) Autonomy: Autonomy means freedom to control one's actions/responses to the environment. Research studies report that jobs that give autonomy to workers also increase sense of responsibility and self esteem. On the contrary, absence or lack of autonomy can cause workers apathy to jobs and, in turn, low and poor performance.

(b) Use of Abilities: Workers perform jobs effectively that offer them opportunity to make use of their abilities. Workers find such jobs as interesting and challenging.

(c) Feedback: Job design should be determined in such a way that workers receive meaningful feedback about what they did. Feedback helps workers improve their performance.

(d) Variety: Lack of variety, or say doing the same work, causes boredom which, in turn, leads to fatigue. Fatigue causes mistakes and accidents. But, by incorporating elements of variety in the job, boredom, fatigue and mistakes can be avoided and the job can be done in more effective and efficient manner.

2.17 Job Design Approaches

Popular approaches of Job Design are Job Enrichment and Job Enlargement.

2.18 Job Enlargement Vs Job Enrichment

Job Enlargement: Job enlargement and job enrichment are both used as techniques for employee motivation and satisfaction. However, they differ a lot from each other. The critical difference is job enlargement is a horizontal expansion of duties and tasks across the same organizational level, whereas job enrichment is the vertical expansion of the roles, responsibilities, authority and activities alongwith the different hierarchical levels. Job enlargement is a technique used for motivating the semi-skilled or unskilled workers and may be misinterpreted as work overload without a good hike in salary. Job enrichment is used for development and satisfaction of the skilled employees which is usually taken as a reward of good work.

Difference and Comparison

Basis	Job enlargement	Job enrichment
1. Meaning	Job enlargement refers to increasing the number of tasks to be performed by an employee to reduce work related boredom.	Job enrichment is that motivational tool which allows more decision making power and work related authority to the employees.
2. Tool / Technique	Job Design Technique	Management Tool
3. Objective/Purpose	Reduce Boredom and Monotony	Make Job Challenging
4. Skills Requirement	No	Yes
5. Expansion	Horizontal	Vertical
6. Level of Responsibility	Remains the Same	Increases
7. Level of Authority	Remains the Same	Increases
8. Directions	Supervisor's Direction	Self-Directed

Basis	Job enlargement	Job enrichment
9. **Dependency on Each Other**	Independent	Dependent
10. **Supervisory Control**	More	Comparatively Less
11. **Result**	Positive or Negative	Usually Positive

Example: Job Enlargement

A person hired to handle the reception work is responsible for handling customer enquiries, queries and calls on the front desk. She kept on doing the same work for two years and got bored. She discussed the problem with the HR manager, who planned to implement job enlargement for making her job profile interesting. Few more tasks were added to her job profile like interacting with the clients and making outbound calls to create new customers for the company. These added tasks reduced her monotony.

Job Enrichment: A Human Resource executive was initially responsible for maintaining the employees' record and calling the candidates for interviews as directed by the HR manager. To add more value to the HR executive's job profile, the manager gave him some authority related to the work already assigned to him. The new responsibilities included providing the employees' provident fund details to the accounts department, keeping contact with the provident fund office and initial scrutinizing of the candidates for the interviews. These additional responsibilities hold authority and accountability, making the employee more efficient, confident and satisfied with the job.

Recruitment

2.19 Introduction

Recruitment is a process of searching and obtaining applicants for jobs. From these applicants appropriate persons can be selected for particular jobs. Theoretically the recruitment process concludes the moment applications for particular job are received. However, practically, recruitment may extend till the process of short listing applications so as to eliminate those who are not qualified for the jobs.

2.20 Purpose or Objectives of Recruitment

- **Determine current and future needs:** To determine the present and future needs of the organization, with the combination of their personal plan and job analysis activities. This is one of the most important objectives of recruitment.
- **Increase in the job pool:** To increase the pool of job candidates at the minimum post cost.
- **Assistance in increasing success rate:** To help increase the success rate of the selection process by reducing the visible number under qualified or exaggerated job applicants.
- **Help reduce the probability:** To help reduce the likelihood of job applicants, once recruited and selected, only after a short period they can cure the organization.
- **Meet the organization's social and legal obligation:** It should fulfill the organization's social and legal liability towards the combination of its employees

- **Start identifying job applicants:** Identifying job applicants and preparing for potential job applicants will be a suitable candidate.
- **Increase effectiveness:** To increase organizational and personal effectiveness in the short-term and long-term.
- **Evaluate effectiveness:** To evaluate the effectiveness of various recruitment techniques, all types of jobs are the source for the applicants. This is the ultimate purpose of recruitment.

2.21 Importance of Recruitment

Recruitment helps organizations in following ways:

- Attract qualified and competent people for the job.
- Ensure that selected applicants stay longer with the organization.
- Make sure that there is match between match between cost and benefit.
- Help the firm create more culturally diverse work-force.

2.22 Sources of Recruitment

The eligible and suitable candidates required for a particular job are available through various sources.

Tata Motors signs MoU to provide employment to Army ex-servicemen

SPECIAL CORRESPONDENT

MUMBAI: Tata Motors has signed a Memorandum of Understanding (MoU) with the Maharashtra Ex-Servicemen Corporation Ltd (MESCO), a government of Maharashtra undertaking, for generate jobs for ex-servicemen of the Indian Army. The MoU is to manufacture certain components for the Future Infantry Combat Vehicle (FICV), a high mobility armoured battle vehicle for infantry men.

$10-billion programme

The $10-billion combat vehicle programme will be developed under the 'Make Category' by Tata Motors and its partners. The FICV will replace the Indian Army's fleet of 2610 Russian-designed BMP (Sarath BMP-II) series armed vehicles that are in operation since 1980.

Ravi Pisharody, Executive Director, Commercial Vehicles, Tata Motors Ltd., said, "Defence particularly needs partners with long-term commitments to see products and solutions through multiple generations of evolution. We have joined hands with MESCO and the Indian army's ex-servicemen for India's first indigenously developed combat vehicle."

"Through this partnership, we will be better positioned to involve the Small & Medium Scale Enterprises in defence equipment manufacturing and cater to the opportunities available in India," he said.

Through this collaboration,

Joins hands with MESCO to build first indigenously developed combat vehicle

Tata Motors plans to utilise the experience of India's ex-servicemen to develop and produce components for the FICV programme.

Vernon Noronha, Vice President, Defence and Government Business, Tata Motors, said: "Aimed at creating skilled professionals in the defence space and in line with the government's 'Make in India' initiative, the collaboration is expected to create domain specific job opportunities for ex-servicemen of the Indian army."

(Retd) Col Suhas Jatkar, Managing Director, MESCO, said, "We are honoured to have partnered with Tata Motors in this unique collaborative effort to generate employment opportunities for the country's ex-servicemen. It will also lead to carving a niche of skilled personnel in the development of defence equipment."

MESCO through its Mahasainik Industrial Estate, India's first unique Ex-servicemen Industrial Estate set-up in Pune in 2002, provides employment to ex-servicemen by undertaking commercial activities close to their homes. Having bagged over 270 contracts so far, MESCO operates in thirty-four districts and employs over 11,000 ex-servicemen.

Sources of Recruitment

Promotions	Press Advertisement
Retirements	Campus Interviews
Former Employees	Placement Agencies
Transfers	Employment Exchange
Internal Advertisement	Walk-in-Interviews
	E-recruitment
	Competitors

Fig. 2.6: Source of Recruitment
Source:https://theintactone.com/2019/03/02/hrm-u2-topic-6-employee-hiring-nature-of-recruitment-sources-of-recruitment/

1. **Internal Sources of Recruitment:**

    (a) **Promotions:** The promotion policy is followed as a motivational technique for the employees who work hard and show good performance. Promotion results in enhancements in pay, position, responsibility and authority. The important requirement for implementation of the promotion policy is that the terms, conditions, rules and regulations should be well-defined.

    (b) **Retirements:** The retired employees may be given the extension in their service in case of non--availability of suitable candidates for the post.

    (c) **Former employees:** Former employees who had performed well during their tenure may be called back, and higher wages and incentives can be paid to them.

    (d) **Transfer:** Employees may be transferred from one department to another wherever the post becomes vacant.

    (e) **Internal advertisement:** The existing employees may be interested in taking up the vacant jobs. As they are working in the company since long time, they know about the specification and description of the vacant job. For their benefit, the advertisement within the company is circulated so that the employees will be intimated.

Benefits of Internal Sources of Recruitment:

1. The existing employees get motivated.
2. Cost is saved as there is no need to give advertisements about the vacancy.
3. It builds loyalty among employees towards the organization.
4. Training cost is saved as the employees already know about the nature of job to be performed.
5. It is a reliable and easy process.

Limitations of Internal Sources of Recruitment:

1. Young people with the knowledge of modern technology and innovative ideas do not get the chance.
2. The performance of the existing employees may not be as efficient as before.
3. It brings the morale down of employees who do not get promotion or selected.
4. It may leads to encouragement to favoritism.
5. It may not be always in the good interest of the organization.

2. **External Sources of Recruitment:**

    (a) **Press Advertisement:** A wide choice for selecting the appropriate candidate for the post is available through this source. It gives publicity to the vacant posts and the details about the job in the form of job description and job specification are made available to public in general.

    (b) **Campus Interviews:** It is the best possible method for companies to select students from various educational institutions. It is easy and economical. The company officials personally visit various institutes and select students eligible for a particular post through interviews. Students get a good opportunity to prove themselves and get selected for a good job.

(c) Placement agencies: A databank of candidates is sent to organizations for their selection purpose and agencies get commission in return.

(d) Employment exchange: People register themselves with government employment exchanges with their personal details. According to the needs and request of the organization, the candidates are sent for interviews.

(e) Walk in interviews: These interviews are declared by companies on the specific day and time and conducted for selection.

(f) E-recruitment: Various sites such as jobs.com, naukri.com, and monster.com are the available electronic sites on which candidates upload their resume and seek the jobs.

(g) Competitors: By offering better terms and conditions of service, the human resource managers try to get the employees working in the competitor's organization.

Benefits of External Sources of Recruitment:

1. New talents get the opportunity.

2. The best selection is possible as a large number of candidates apply for the job.

3. In case of unavailability of suitable candidates within the organization, it is better to select them from outside sources.

Limitations of External Sources of Recruitment:

1. Skilled and ambitious employees may switch the job more frequently.

2. It gives a sense of insecurity among the existing candidates.

3. It increases the cost as advertisement is to be given through press and training facilities to be provided for new candidates.

2.23 Difference between Recruitment and Selection

Sr. No.	Recruitment	Selection
1.	Recruitment is the process of searching the candidates for employment and stimulating them to apply for jobs in the organization.	Selection involves the series of steps by which the candidates are screened for choosing the most suitable persons for vacant posts.
2.	The basic purpose of Recruitment is to create a talent pool of candidates to enable the selection of best candidates for the organization, by attracting more and more employees to apply in the organization.	The basic purpose of Selection process is to choose the right candidate to fill the various positions in the organization.

Sr. No.	Recruitment	Selection
3.	Recruitment is a positive process i.e. encouraging more and more employees to apply.	Selection is a negative process as it involves rejection of the unsuitable candidates.
4.	Recruitment is concerned with tapping the sources of human resources.	Selection is concerned with selecting the most suitable candidate through various interviews and tests.
5.	There is no contract of recruitment established in recruitment.	Selection results in a contract of service between the employer and the selected employee.

(Adapted from: https://www.linkedin.com/pulse/difference-between-recruitment-process-selection-sarika-chebrolu)

Selection

2.24 Meaning

Selection is the process of differentiating between the applications received for the job in order to identify and hire those with higher chances of being successful in a job.

2.25 Process of Selection

The selection process varies from industry to industry, company to company and even amongst departments of the same company. The selection procedure comprises of following systematic steps which are described in Figure 2.7.

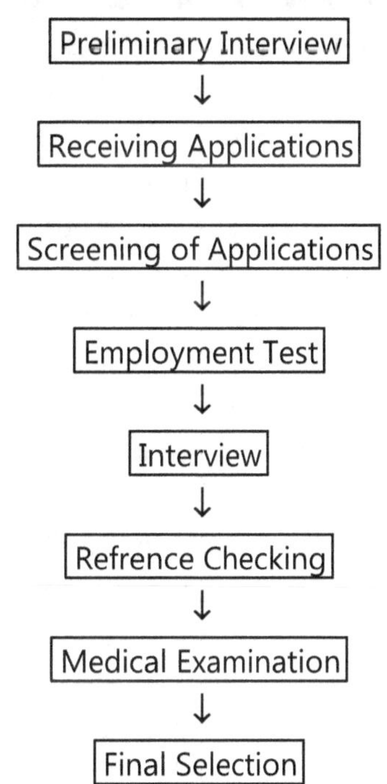

Fig. 2.7: Selection Procedures

Source: https://businessjargons.com/selection-process.html

1. **Preliminary Interview:** The preliminary interview is also called as a screening interview wherein those candidates are eliminated from the further selection process who do not meet the minimum eligibility criteria as required by the organization. Here, the individuals are checked for their academic qualifications, skill sets, family backgrounds and their interest in working with the firm. The preliminary interview is less formal and is basically done to weed out the unsuitable candidates very much before proceeding with a full-fledged selection process.

2. **Receiving Applications:** Once the candidate qualifies the preliminary interview; he is required to fill in the application form in the prescribed format. This application contains the candidate data such as age, qualification, experience, etc. This information helps the interviewer to get the fair idea about the candidate and formulate questions to get more information about him.

3. **Screening of Applications:** Once the applications are received, these are screened by the screening committee, who then prepare a list of those applicants whom they find suitable for the interviews. The short listing criteria could be the age, sex, qualification, experience of an individual. Once the list is prepared, the qualified candidates are called for the interview either through a registered mail or e-mails.

4. **Employment Tests:** In order to check the mental ability and skill set of an individual, several tests are conducted. Such as intelligence tests, aptitude tests, interest tests, psychological tests, personality tests, etc. These tests are conducted to judge the suitability of the candidate for the job.

5. **Employment Interview:** The one on one session with the candidate is conducted to gain more insights about him. Here, the interviewer asks questions to the applicant to discover more about him and to give him the accurate picture of the kind of a job he is required to perform. Also, the briefing of certain organizational policies is done, which is crucial in the performance of the job. Through an interview, it is easier for the employer to understand the candidate's expectations from the job and also his communication skills alongwith the confidence level can be checked at this stage.

6. **Checking References:** The firms usually ask for the references from the candidate to cross check the authenticity of the information provided by him. These references could be from the education institute from where the candidate has completed his studies or from his previous employment where he was formerly engaged. These references are checked to know the conduct and behavior of an individual and also his potential of learning new jobs.

7. **Medical Examination:** Here the physical and mental fitness of the candidate are checked to ensure that he is capable of performing the job. In some organizations,

the medical examination is done at the very beginning of the selection process while in some cases it is done after the final selection. Thus, this stage is not rigid and can take place anywhere in the process. The medical examination is an important step in the selection process as it helps in ascertaining the applicant's physical ability to fulfil the job requirements.

8. **Final Selection:** Finally, the candidate who qualifies all the rounds of a selection process is given the appointment letter to join the firm.

Thus, the selection is complex and a lengthy process as it involves several stages that an individual has to qualify before getting finally selected for the job.

Induction and Orientation

Both induction and orientation are inter-related processes that refer to an instigation programme designed to help new employees to adjust to an organization. The two words induction and orientation are often used interchangeably, even though there is a difference between them based on meaning and application. The main difference between induction and orientation is that induction refers to a process of introducing the newcomer to his company and work environment whereas orientation is the process of helping the newcomer to align with his new position, responsibilities and work culture.

2.26 Induction

The term induction comes from the Latin *'inducere'*, meaning to bring in or introduce. Just as the origins suggest, induction is a kind of an introduction. Induction is the process of formally admitting someone to a post or an organization. It is the process of introducing a new employee to the organization and vice versa. In this stage, the new employee learns how to become a part of the organization.

Induction can include making the newcomer aware of the organizational hierarchy and company overview. So it can include information like mission, vision, objectives, history of the company, clients, policies and dress code, etc. Induction has a shorter duration and can be conducted on the day the new employee joins the organization itself. Induction can be conducted through video sessions or PowerPoint presentation.

2.27 Orientation

Orientation is a process that aims at helping the new employee to adjust to his department, position, responsibilities and work culture. It is a more of a formal programme following induction. The duration of the orientation session can vary from one to several days depending on the needs of the organization as well as the department. During the orientation session, the newcomer will learn about his assignments, team members, various procedures, and processes, etc. The new employee is made to familiarize himself with the work environment, equipment and the tasks he is expected to perform. The process of induction and orientation can vary from one organization to another, but the aim of any induction or orientation programme is to facilitate a smooth transition of an employee into his new environment.

Difference between Induction and Orientation:

Parameter	Induction	Orientation
1. **Meaning**	Induction refers to a process of introducing the newcomer to his company and work environment.	Orientation is the process of helping the newcomer to align with his new position, responsibilities and work culture.
2. **Type of information**	Induction can contain information like company overview, organizational hierarchy, policies etc.	Orientation can provide information like the new employee's assignments, team members, various procedures, and processes etc.
3. **Duration**	Induction has a short duration. It can be completed in a day.	Orientation has a longer duration. It can take one to several days depending on the organizational requirements.
4. **Formality level**	Induction can be more informal than orientation.	Orientation can be more formal than induction.
5. **Order**	Induction is the first process.	Orientation comes after induction.

Career Planning

2.28 Career Planning: Definition

Career planning is the process of enhancing an employee's future value.

According to Schermerborn, Hunt, and Osborn, 'Career planning is a process of systematically matching career goals and individual capabilities with opportunities for their fulfillment'.

2.29 Features of Career Planning and Career Development

1. It is an ongoing process.
2. It helps individuals develop skills required to fulfill different career roles.

3. It strengthens work-related activities in the organization.

4. It defines life, career, abilities, and interests of the employees.

5. It can also give professional directions, as they relate to career goals.

2.30 Process of Career Planning

1. **Analyzing Employee Needs and Aspirations:** Sometimes, most of the employees do not know their career anchors and aspirations. Organizations also assume the career goals and aspirations of employees which need not be in tune with the reality. Therefore, first of all, an analysis of the employee career anchors, aspirations and goals must be done through objective assessment. This assessment is based on personnel inventory. Since most employees do not have a clear idea of their career anchors and aspirations, they, therefore, need to be provided as much information about these matters as possible informing what kind of work would suit the employee most considering his/her skills, experience and aptitude into account.

2. **Analyzing Career Opportunities:** Once career aspirations and goals of employee are known, there is a need to analyze various career opportunities available to offer under prevailing career paths in the organization. Career paths indicate career progression. Here also, since many employees may not be aware of their own career progression path, this needs to be made known to them. Sometimes organizations may offer career progression at a particular level for both young direct recruits and own older employees through promotions. Recognizing varying kinds of career anchors and aspirations of the two types of employees, organizations need to outline career paths striking a balance between those of internal employees with experience but without professional degree and those new recruits with excellent professional degree but lacking experience.

3. **Identifying Congruence and Incongruence:** At this stage, a mechanism for identifying congruence between employee career aspirations and organizational career system is developed. This helps identify specific areas where mismatch or incongruence prevails. This is done through relating different jobs to different career opportunities. Such a mechanism of match and mismatch between career aspirations and opportunities enables the organization to develop realistic career goals, both long-term and short-term.

4. **Action Plans and Periodic Review:** Having identified the mismatch, now it is necessary to formulate an alternative strategy to deal with the same.

Succession Planning

2.31 Definition

Succession planning is a process by which individuals are observed to pass on the leadership role within a company. The process ensures that business continues to operate efficiently without the presence of people who were holding key positions as they must have retired, resigned, etc.

Succession Planning, specifically termed as Management Succession Planning, involves coaching and development of prospective successors or people within a firm or from outside to take up key positions in an organization through an organized process of assessment and training.

It ensures a smooth transition of power in key leadership roles. If the successor is chosen within the organization, it will help motivate the employees, and also save on cost and extra time which the management would have spent in scanning candidates from other firms.

2.32 Process of Succession Planning

There are four main stages in the succession planning process, which involve transition (movement of new role), initiation, selection, and education.

1. **'Transition':** In this phase, the business owner or the CEO retires or moves out of the organization, and the chosen successor formally takes up the responsibility as his/her new leadership role

2. **'Initiations':** In this stage, potential candidates for the job learn about the business, more importantly about its value system, guidelines, values, vision, etc. Here the CEO or any top leader of the organization talks about these key things to the candidates.

3. **'Selection':** It is a complex task, where a specific candidate is chosen to be a successor among other candidates who were running for the same job.

4. **'Training and Education':** It involves an exhaustive training scheduled for the successor so that he can meet the goals of the organization as well as returns for the shareholders.

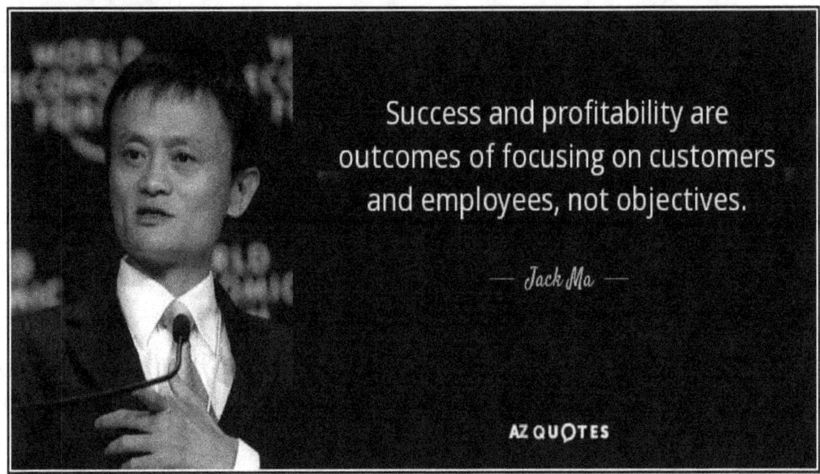

Jack Ma – Alibaba

Jack Ma was the kinetic leader of Alibaba, who grew the world's largest e-commerce company that has a market cap of $240 million. He successfully grew the company over a 15 year period and much of his success has been attributed to his management style, where he blended Eastern and Western management and technology practices. One of the key traits of Jack Ma is that he surrounded himself with successful and valuable people. His approach was to empower those successful people within his company and allow them to control and develop the business in accordance with his vision. Additionally, he created a culture of participation, energy, and fun. This allowed Alibaba to retain loyal and hardworking staff that would ultimately build the success of Alibaba.

Retention of Employees

2.33 Meaning

Employee retention refers to the various policies and practices which let the employees stick to an organization for a longer period of time. Every organization invests time and money to groom a new joinee, make him a corporate ready material and bring him at par with the existing employees. The organization is completely at loss when the employees leave their job once they are fully trained. Employee retention takes into account the various measures taken so that an individual stays in an organization for the maximum period of time.

2.34 Need and Importance of Employee Retention

Let us understand why retaining a valuable employee is essential for an organization.

1. **Hiring is not an easy process:** The HR Professional shortlists few individuals from a large pool of talent, conducts preliminary interviews and eventually forwards it to the respective line managers who further grill them to judge whether they are fit for the organization or not. Recruiting the right candidate is a time consuming process.

2. **An organization invests time and money in grooming an individual and makes him ready to work and understand the corporate culture:** A new joinee is completely raw and the management really has to work hard to train him for his overall development. It is a complete wastage of time and money when an individual leaves an organization all of a sudden. The HR has to start the recruitment process all over again for the same vacancy; a mere duplication of work. Finding a right employee for an organization is a tedious job and all efforts simply go waste when the employee leaves.

3. **When an individual resigns from his present organization, it is more likely that he would join the competitors:** In such cases, employees tend to take all the strategies, policies from the current organization to the new one. Individuals take all the important data, information and statistics to their new organization and in some cases even leak the secrets of the previous organization. To avoid such cases, it is essential that the new joinee is made to sign a document which stops him from passing on any information even if he leaves the organization. Strict policy should be made which prevents the employees to join the competitors. This is an effective way to retain the employees.

4. **The employees working for a longer period of time are more familiar with the company's policies, guidelines and thus they adjust better:** They perform better than individuals who change jobs frequently. Employees who spend a considerable time in an organization know the organization in and out and thus are in a position to contribute effectively.

5. **Every individual needs time to adjust with others:** One needs time to know his team members well, be friendly with them and eventually trust them. Organizations are always benefited when the employees are compatible with each other and discuss things among themselves to come out with something beneficial for all. When a new individual replaces an existing employee, adjustment problems crop up. Individuals find it really difficult to establish a comfort level with the other person. After striking a rapport with an existing employee, it is a challenge for the employees to adjust with someone new and most importantly trust him. It is a human tendency to compare a new joinee with the previous employees and always find faults in him.

6. **It has been observed that individuals sticking to an organization for a longer span are more loyal towards the management and the organization:** They enjoy all kinds of benefits from the organization and as a result are more attached to it. They hardly badmouth their organization and always think in favour of the management. For them the organization comes first and all other things later.

7. **It is essential for the organization to retain the valuable employees showing potential:** Every organization needs hardworking and talented employees who can really come out with something creative and different. No organization can survive if all the top performers quit. It is essential for the organization to retain those employees who really work hard and are indispensable for the system. The management must understand the difference between a valuable employee and an employee who doesn't contribute much to the organization. Sincere efforts must be made to encourage the employees so that they stay happy in the current organization and do not look for a change.

2.35 Employee Retention Strategies

Every area of the employer-employee relationship in your organization deserves your attention. Embrace these key strategies to improve your organization's employee retention and boost employee satisfaction:

1. **On boarding and Orientation:** Every new hire should be set-up for success from the very start, from the first day of work to the first week and beyond. The job orientation is just one component of on boarding, which can last for weeks or months, depending on your organization. Aim to develop an on boarding process where new staff members not only learn about the job but also the company culture and how they can contribute and thrive, with on-going discussions, goals and opportunities to address questions and issues as they arrive.

2. **Mentorship Programmes:** Pairing a new employee with a mentor is a great idea for onboarding. New team members can learn the ropes from a veteran with a wealth of resources, and the new hire offers a fresh viewpoint to experienced staff. Mentors shouldn't be work supervisors, but they can offer guidance and be a sounding board for newcomers, welcoming them into the company culture.

3. **Employee Compensation:** It's absolutely essential in this competitive labor market for companies to offer attractive compensation packages. That includes salaries, of course, but also bonuses, paid time off, health benefits, retirement plans and all the other perks that can distinguish one workplace from another. Every employee should have a full understanding of all the benefits they receive from your organization.

4. **Recognition and Rewards Systems:** Every person wants to feel appreciated for what they do. Make it a habit to thank your direct reports when they go the extra mile, whether it's with a sincere email, a gift card or an extra day off. Show your

employees you appreciate them, and share how their hard work helps the organization. Some companies set-up rewards systems that incentivize great ideas and innovation, but you can institute recognition programmes even on a small team with a small budget.

5. **Work-life Balance:** What message is your company culture sending? If staff are expected to regularly work long hours and be at your beck and call, you'll likely run into issues with employee retention. Burnout is real. A healthy work-life balance is essential, and people need to know that management understands its importance. Encourage staff to take vacation time, and if late nights are necessary to wrap up a project, see if you can offer late arrivals or an extra day off to compensate and increase job satisfaction. Many companies offer telecommuting or flexible schedules to improve work-life balance for their employees.

6. **Training and Development:** In any position and industry, professionals want the possibility for advancement. Smart managers invest in their workers' professional development and seek opportunities for them to grow. Ask each of your direct reports about their short- and long-term goals to determine how you can help achieve them. Some companies pay for employees to attend conferences or industry events each year, or provide tuition reimbursement or continuing education training.

7. **Communication and Feedback:** Keeping open lines of communication are essential for employee retention. Your direct reports should feel that they can come to you with ideas, questions and concerns, and likewise, they expect you to be honest and open with them about improvements they need to make in their own performance. Make sure you connect with each staff member on a regular basis — don't let issues build up for the annual review.

8. **Dealing with Change:** Every workplace has to deal with unpleasant changes occasionally, and the staff looks to leadership for reassurance. If your organization is going through a merger, layoffs or other big changes, keep your staff informed as much as you can to avoid feeding the rumour mill. Make big announcements face to face, and make sure you allow time for their questions.

9. **Fostering Teamwork:** When people work together, they can achieve more than they would have individually. Foster a culture of collaboration that accommodates individuals' working styles and lets their talents shine. Do this by clarifying team objectives, business goals and roles, and encouraging everyone to contribute ideas and solutions.

10. **Team Celebration:** Celebrate major milestones for individuals and for the team. Whether the team just finished that huge quarterly project under budget or an employee brought home a new baby, seize the chance to celebrate together with a shared meal or group excursion.

Transfers and Promotions

2.36 Introduction to Transfer

One of the internal mobility of the employee is transfer. It is lateral movement of employee in an organization. Transfers of employees are quite common in all organizations. In simple words "Transfer" refers to a change in job assignment of an employee" or "A Horizontal shifting of an employee from one job to another without any job related increase in pay, benefits and status of the employees."

In Transfers there is no change in the responsibility, designation, status or salary. It is the process of employee's adjustment with the work, time and place. It may also be made as disciplinary action. Transfer may be initiated either by the company or the employee. In practice, the company may transfer the employee to the place where he/she can prove more useful and effective. Similarly, employee may initiate transfer to a location where he/she is likely to enjoy greater satisfaction.

Transfer could be permanent, temporary or ad hoc to meet emergencies. Usually, permanent transfers are made due to changes in work load or death, retirement, resignation, etc. of some employee. As regards temporary transfer, it arises mainly due to ill health, absenteeism, etc. of some employee.

Transfer decisions may be seemed as negative or positive depending upon an individual's personal preferences, needs and aspirations.

For example, an organisation may consider transfer from Guwahati regional office to Delhi-head office as positive and reward because it will enable the employee to broaden his/her knowledge and work experience. On the contrary, the employee may look down upon it as it breaks ties with his people and community in Guwahati.

Thus we may define Transfer as an employee's lateral mobility in the organization structure without any significant change in the authority, responsibility, compensation and social status.

2.37 Need of Transfer

The need for making transfer is left for various reasons as listed below:

1. **To Meet Organizational Needs:** Changes in technology, volume of production, production schedule, product line, quality of products, organisational structure, etc. necessitate an organisation to re-assign jobs among employees so that right employee is placed on the right job.

2. **To Satisfy Employee Needs:** Employee may request for transfer in order to satisfy their desire to work in the particular department, place and under some superior boss. Personal problems of an employee may also results in transfer.

3. **To Better Utilize Employee:** When an employee is not performing satisfactorily on one job and management thinks that his/her capabilities would be utilized better elsewhere, he/she may be transferred to other job.

4. **To Make the Employee More Versatile:** In some organisations like banks, employees after working on a job for a specified period are transferred to other job with a view to widen their knowledge and skill and also reduce monotony. This is also called 'job rotation.

5. **To Adjust the Workforce:** Work force can be transferred from the departments / plants where there is less work to the departments/plants where the work is more.

6. **To Provide Relief:** Transfers may be made to give relief to the employees who are overburdened or doing hazardous work for long period.

7. **To Punish Employee:** Management may use Transfer as an instrument to punish employees who are involved in various undesirable activities. They are transferred to any remote areas as a part of disciplinary action.

2.38 Definitions of Transfers

- *According to Edwin Flippo, a Transfer*, *"is a change in job where the new job is substantially equal to the old in terms of pay, status and responsibilities".*

- **Yoder and Associates have defined transfer as**, *"a lateral shift causing movement of individuals from one position to another usually without involving any marked change in duties, responsibilities, skills needed or compensation".*

- **According to Dale Yoder**, *"A transfer involves the shifting of an employee from any job to another without special reference to change responsibility or compensation".*

- **According to Policy Manual-University of North Texas Transfer is defined as**, *" the permanent lateral movement of a staff member from one position to another position in the same or another job class assigned to the same salary range".*

2.39 Types of Transfer

1. **Inter-Departmental v/s Intra-Departmental Transfer:** When employees are rotated from one job to another within the same department, it is called Intra-Departmental Transfer. *For example, when a clerk in a bank branch is made an accountant and if both the jobs carries equal levels of responsibilities and compensation then it is Intra-Departmental Transfer.* While on the other hand, when employees are moved from one department to another within the same job classification, it is Inter-Departmental Transfer.

2. **Voluntary v/s Involuntary Transfer:** When an employee voluntarily applies for a transfer to some other various position or place within the same job classification, it

is called a voluntary transfer. An employee may request for a transfer to another position within or outside the department. Involuntary Transfer refers to transfer of an employee by the organization for administrative or for some other reasons without their concurrence. *For example, an organization may transfer an employee when his existing position or job is marked to be end due to restructuring process.*

3. **Replacement Transfer:** It refers to movement of an employee within an organization to replace an existing employee. It is an infrequent type of transfer.

4. **Versatility Transfer:** Versatility means possessing wide variety of skills. Such type of transfers may help an employee to acquire different types of skills required to perform the jobs in higher positions in the organization. *For example, an Entry Level Manager may be trained in different positions with equivalent responsibilities and duties ahead of their promotion to the higher levels of management.*

5. **Shift Transfer:** This is done in organization when there are multiple shifts involved. In this method an employee are transferred from one shift to another but will remain in the same job. For *example, an employee may be transferred from day shift to night shift.* It is done on rotation basis or request basis.

6. **Remedial Transfer:** It refers to transfer which are usually carried out to set right the past mistakes in the appointment or transfer concerning an employee. Wrong recruitment of an employee may cause problems for both organization as well as employees themselves. To rectify such situations, organizations usually way out to remedial transfers which enable employees to find the right job and right environment.

7. **Production Transfers:** It refers to movement of employees within an organization due to changes in production requirements.

2.40 Introduction and Definitions of Promotion

Promotion can be defined as the advancement of an employee from one position to another which results in financial benefits. It is certainly good motivator for employees as it boost their morale. Organizations use Promotion as a tool to enhance the performance of employees as well as to reward them according to the merit and their sincerity towards work. Internal promotion of an employee increases his loyalty towards the organization. Promotion which are normally accompanied by financial incentives , also fulfill the economic needs of the employees, in addition to fulfilling the social need of attaining increased status in the society. In fact, Promotion has an in built motivational value as it lifts up the authority, status and power of an employee within the organization. It is considered as good personnel policy to fill vacancy in higher jobs through promotion from within because such promotions provide motivation to employees and also removes their feelings of frustration.

Advancement in the career of a employee is the essence of the definitions of promotion. We shall now see the definitions of Promotions which are as follows:

- **According to Pigours and Myers,** *'Promotion is advancement of an employee to a better job – better in terms of greater responsibility, more prestige or status, greater skill and especially increased rate of pay or salary".*

- **According to Arun Monappa and Mirza S Saiyadain defined promotion as** *"the upward re-assignment of an individual in an organization's hierarchy, accompanied by increased responsibilities, enhanced status and usually with increased income though not always so".*

- **According to Wendell French,** *"Promotion is a type of transfer which involves re-assignment of an employee to a higher position, having higher pay, more privileges and increased benefits"*

Thus we may defined Promotion as an employee's upward mobility in the organizational structure accompanied by increased in authority, responsibility, compensation and social status also.

2.41 Need for Promotion

1. To recognize employee's performance and commitment.
2. To motivate him towards better performance.
3. To develop competitive spirit among employees for acquiring knowledge and skills for higher level jobs.
4. To retain skilled and talented employees.
5. To reduce discontent and unrest.
6. To fill up job's vacant position that is created due to retirement, resignation or demise of an employee. In this case, next senior employee will be promoted to the vacant job.
7. To utilize more effectively the knowledge and skills of employees; and
8. To attract suitable and competent employees.

2.42 Types of Promotion

1. **Horizontal Promotions:** It brings more responsibility and compensation but the employee does not go to a higher level in the organizational structure. This method of promotion is usually adopted when the chances of going up in the organizational structure are limited. It is generally viewed as an element of an employee's career growth.
2. **Vertical Promotions:** Generally Promotion means going up in the organizational structure or ladder. A Vertical Promotion indicates the advancement of an employee to higher positions in the organization. It is accompanied by increased authority, responsibility, status and higher designation.

3. **Dry Promotions:** It refers to increase in responsibility and status of an employee without any increase in pay or other financial benefits.

4. **Open/Closed System of Promotions:** In case of Open promotions, an organization does not limit promotional opportunities to any particular section of employees. On the contrary it keeps them open to all the eligible employees. In practice, all vacancies are openly advertised within the organization and applications are invited from all who fulfil the eligibility conditions prescribed by the organization. In contrast, the closed system restricts the promotional opportunities to select list of employees. In this method, employees get promotion through closed promotional recruitment system established by the organization.

Points to remember

1. Human Resource Planning is basically the process of identifying the right person for the right job at the right time and at the right cost.

2. Objectives of HRP are Achieve Goal, Estimates future organizational structure and Manpower Requirements, Human Resource Audit, Job analysis.

3. Need of HRP are Shortage of skills, Changing needs of technology, Changes in organisation design and structure.

4. The Steps in HR Planning process are Analysing Organizational Objectives, Inventory of Present Human Resources, Forecasting Demand and Supply of Human Resource, Estimating Manpower Gaps, Formulating the Human Resource Action Plan, Monitoring, Control and Feedback.

5. The Barriers to the HR planning process are Resistance by Employers, Resistance by Employees, and Inadequacies in quality of information, uncertainties, Time and expense.

6. Job analysis is a process of gathering relevant information about various aspects of a job including its content and the job performer's skill requirements.

7. The uses of Job analysis are Human resource planning, Recruitment and Selection, Training and development, Remuneration, Performance Appraisal, Health and safety.

8. The steps in Job analysis are: Organizational analysis, Select representative positions, Collect data, Review collected data, Developing Job Description, Developing Job Specification.

9. Job description is a written statement that describes all the aspects of a job.

10. Components of Job Description are Job title, Job location, Role, Responsibilities and duties, Salary, Incentives and Allowances.

11. Job specification is a document which specifies the minimum acceptable qualities required for a person to complete the job satisfactorily.

12. Components of Job Specification are Educational Qualification, Skills, and Experience.

13. Job Design is basically a combination of the job content and the work method adopted in the job.

14. Techniques of Job Design are Job specification, Job Enrichment, Job rotation and Job Enlargement.

15. Factors affecting Job Design are: Organizational, Environmental, Behavioural

16. Recruitment refers to search for promising job applicants to fill vacancies that may arise in an organization.

17. Organizations have two sources of recruitment: One is Internal Recruitment which refers to filling open with the current employees of the organization and the other external recruitment refers to reaching out to external labour market   to meet the requirements.

18. Examples of Internal Recruitment are Promotions, Retirement, Former Employees, Transfer and Internal Advertisement while examples of External recruitment are Press advertisement, Campus interview, Placement agencies, Employment exchanges, Walk in interviews, E-recruitment, Competitors.

19. Selection is the process of differentiating between the applications received for the job in order to identify and hire those with higher chances of being successful in a job.

20. Steps involved in Selection are Preliminary Interview, Receiving applications, Screening Applications, Employment Tests, Employment Interview, Checking References, Medical Examinations, Final Selection.

21. Induction is the process of formally admitting someone to a post or an organization. It is the process of introducing a new employee to the organization and vice versa. While Orientation is a process that aims at helping the new employee to adjust to his department, position, responsibilities and work culture. It is a more of a formal programme following induction.

22. Career planning is the process of enhancing an employee's future value. The Process of career planning includes Analyzing employee needs and aspirations, Analyzing career opportunities, Identifying congruence and incongruence, Action plans and periodic review

23. Succession planning is a process by which individuals are observed to pass on the leadership role within a company.

24. The steps involved in Succession Planning are: Transition (movement of new role), initiation, Selection, and Training and education.
25. Employee retention refers to the various policies and practices which let the employees stick to an organization for a longer period of time.
26. Transfers refer to "A Horizontal shifting of an employee from one job to another without any job related increase in pay, benefits and status of the employees."
27. Types of Transfer are Inter-Departmental v/s Intra-Departmental Transfer, Voluntary v/s Involuntary Transfer, Replacement Transfer, Versatility Transfer, Shift Transfer, Remedial Transfer and Production Transfers.
28. Promotion can be defined as the advancement of an employee from one position to another which results in financial benefits. Types of Promotions are Horizontal Promotions, Vertical Promotions, Dry Promotions, Open/Closed System of Promotions.

Skills Development Exercise for Students

Objective: The objective of this exercise is to show you how to conduct environmental scanning to understand the changes in the external factors and to develop an appropriate HR plans based on the analysis of the Internal and External situation of the organization.

Procedure Note: The class is divided into groups. Each group has (1) An HR Manager, (2) 2 HR Team Members (3) 2 HR Experts from outside the organization (4) 2 Observers of the meeting (5) 2 union representatives. The role of the observer is to observe and report on various aspects of the role playing sessions

Situation: Rathosh International Limited is a leading company dealing with the production of polyester fabrics. The Company has shown a steady performance for the past several decades. It has a commendable HR team with an excellent track record in employee productivity and satisfaction. The HR department has also succeeded in maintaining a long period of Industrial peace and harmony. The company has strong work culture with clear emphasis on commitment, competency, and consistency. Its HR policy is aligned closely with its corporate strategy.

In such situation the management of the company recently came up with the decision to diversify its operation drastically. As a first step in the process of diversification, it decided to enter the field of telecommunications in a big way. After making necessary budgetary provisions, the Company directed the HR Department to develop an HR plans for implementing this proposal. It instructed the HR department to undertake an extensive survey of economic and industrial environment and forecast the HR requirements and availability accordingly. The whole part was aim at optimizing the labour cost.

> **Steps in the Exercise: There are 3 steps to the exercise:**
>
> Step 1: The HR Manager meets the external HR experts to assess the developments in the external environment of the organization and their implications for the HR plans.
>
> Step 2: The HR Manager conducts talks with the union representative to ascertain the internal situation of the firm.
>
> Step 3: The HR Manager convenes a meeting attended by the 2 HR team members to develop an appropriate HR plan. The Plan would be then sent to the top management for approval.
>
> Step 4: Observers will have to analyze and provide feedback on the performance of the members in the role playing session.

Questions for Discussion

1. What is Human Resource planning? Explain the objectives, need and importance of it?
2. Explain the process of Human Resource planning.
3. What is Job analysis? Explain the process of it.
4. Explain the contents of Job Analysis.
5. What is Job design and its factors affecting it?
6. Distinguish between Job Enrichment and Job Enlargement?
7. What is Recruitment? Explain the steps in the process of Recruitment.
8. Discuss the various Sources of Recruitment.
9. You have been appointed as the HR Manager of Renaissance Industries Limited, Chennai. It proposes to select management trainees for its different departments. What sources should it explore and how should the trainees be selected?
10. Evaluate critically the steps in the Selection Process.
11. Define the term Induction and Orientation in your own words.
12. Evaluate critically the Career Planning process with relevant examples.
13. What is Succession Planning? Explain the process of it.
14. What is Transfer? Explain its types with relevant examples.
15. Discuss the meaning of Promotion with its need and types.
16. What is Retention? Explain its importance.
17. What are the strategies used to retain an employees in an organization?

Questions from Previous MBA Examinations

1. What is Human Resource planning? Explain the process of HRP in your own language. **(April 2016)**

Ans. Refer Articles 2.1, 2.2 and 2.6 of this chapter.

2. What is Job Analysis? Explain its importance and purpose. **(April 2016)**

Ans. Refer Articles 2.9, 2.10 and 2.11 of this chapter.

3. Explain various steps of Human Resource planning and discuss briefly various sources of recruitment. **(November 2016)**

Ans. Refer Articles 2.6 and 2.22 of this chapter.

4. What is Career Planning? What are the stages of Career Planning? **(April 2017)**

Ans. Refer Articles 2.28 and 2.30 of this chapter.

5. What are the various internal and external Sources of Recruitment?

(November 2017)

Ans. Refer Article 2.22 of this chapter.

6. Define HRP. Explain the objectives and benefits. **(April 2018)**

Ans. Refer Articles 2.2, 2.3 and 2.5 of this chapter.

7. What is Job Design? Explain the factors affecting Job Design. **(April 2018)**

Ans. Refer Articles 2.15 and 2.16 of this chapter.

Case Study: (Efficiency of Selection Process vis-à-vis Labour Turnover)

Relyon is an insurance company with branches all over India. All the HR activities of the company are carried out by the HR professionals based at the headquarters of the company located in New Delhi. The hiring practice of the company is that the HR staff at the central office recruits the personnel for the managerial cadre for all its branches and leaves the recruitment of other cadres to the managers in charge of their respective branches. The company recently opened a branch at Rameswaram in Tamil Nadu.

Amitabh, the General Manager (HR) posted Arvind as the manager for the recently opened branch. In conformity with the company's hiring practice, Arvind recruited other personnel for his branch. But within one year of its operation, this branch witnessed a high labour turnover. The turnover rate was much higher than the company's overall average of 10 percent. Posts like accounts officer turned over four times while computer operators worked only for a few months and this was the case with the salespeople, who on an average lasted only for a few months. The head office took serious view, of these developments.

The Branch manager was called to the HR department of the Head Office to explain the reasons for such high labour turnover in his office. Amitabh, the HR General Manager asked Arvind about the hiring practices adopted by the latter for choosing employees for his branch. Arvind explained that he made an initial assessment of the candidate on the basis of the data provided by them in their applications forms. Those who met the minimum criteria set for the job were then called for an unstructured Interview. During the interview the candidates were asked questions relevant to their field to measure their knowledge, skills and proficiency in the job.

Arvind mentioned that he observed the candidate's sitting posture, how he presented himself, his initial remarks, his mannerism, and also his overall attire. These factors had a decisive influence on his final assessment of the candidate. The candidate was also quizzed about his real intentions for joining this company and also his career plans. Finally a ranked list was prepared on the basis of performance in Interview and job offer was given to the selected candidates.

Amitabh who listened attentively to Arvind was neither satisfied nor dissatisfied with Arvind's explanation but began to think about the possible role of the selection process in contributing to the high labour turnover.

Questions:

1. What is your opinion about the hiring policy adopted by Relyon?

2. What is your assessment about the hiring practices adopted by Arvind?

3. State the recommendations you would like to make to Arvind for improving his hiring practices?

References

1. Bulla, D N and Scott, P M (1994) Manpower requirements forecasting: a case example, in Human Resource Forecasting and Modelling, ed D Ward, T P Bechet and R Tripp, Human Resource Planning Society, New York

2. Reilly, P., (2003). Guide to Workforce Planning in Local Authorities, Employers Organization for Local Government, London.

3. Bajracharya, S. (2018) "Job Analysis: Definitions, Methods, Process and Importance of Job Analysis," in Businesstopia, Available at https://www.businesstopia.net/human-resource/ job-analysis-definitions-methods-process-importance.

4. Human Resource Management - Pearson Book.

Chapter **3**...

Managing Employee Performance and Training

Contents ...

Learning Objectives:

> ➢ Define the terms of Performance Appraisal and Performance Management.
> ➢ Define and Learn importance of Performance Appraisal and Performance Management.
> ➢ Understand the process, methods and purpose of it.
> ➢ Define and understand the difference between Training and Development
> ➢ Examine Types and Models of Training.
> ➢ Understand the nature and importance of Training and Development

---

Opening Vignettes/Pragmatic Insights: The Aditya Birla Group is an Indian Multinational Conglomerate, headquartered in Worli, Mumbai, Maharashtra India. It operates in 34 countries with more than 1, 20,000 employees worldwide. It has vast and diverse business interests. The group has several innovative HR initiatives that aim at treating the employees as a group resource. Acknowledging employees through Aditya Birla Awards for outstanding performance has been one of its major Employee engagement programmes The Aditya Birla Group views a transparent performance management process as a vital employee retention tool. The main features of its Performance Management Process include pre- determined goals and key result areas (KRAs) to enable the employees to know what is expected from them, a midyear review, an annual performance appraisal process which includes self-assessment, supervisor assessment and a skip level review, an assessment of an individual on values compliance and demonstration and finally a documentation of career aspirations along with the development requirements to achieve those aspirations. The Aditya Birla Group proves that the companies can make rapid pace with an efficient performance management which we shall discuss in this chapter.

3.1 Introduction to Performance Appraisal and Performance Management

"Performance" defined by Bates and Holton as "multidimensional context, the measurement of which varies, depending on variety of factors". In simple sense Performance is all about how things are done as well as what is done. It is the degree of accomplishment of the tasks of a particular job. It reflects how much and how the requirements of the job have been fulfilled. Performance is always measured in terms of results. Today the Role of HR has undergone a sea change and its focus is on evolving such functional strategies which enable successful implementation of the major corporate strategies. In a way, HR and corporate strategies function in alignment. Today, HR works towards facilitating and improving the performance of the employees by building a conducive work environment and providing maximum opportunities to the employees for participating in organizational planning and decision making process. Today, all the major activities of HR are driven towards development of high performance leaders and fostering employee motivation. So, it can be interpreted that the role of HR has evolved from merely an appraiser to a facilitator and an enabler.

Usually, ***Performance Management*** and ***Performance Appraisal*** are used interchangeably. They may have some similarities but they are definitely not the same! For one, Performance Management is a comprehensive approach that involves the maximum amount of dialogue among all the stakeholders. Performance appraisal on the other hand is primarily a top-down assessment for grading/rating employee's performance periodically.

Performance Management is an HRM process concerned with getting the best performance from individuals in an organization as well as getting the best performance from the teams, and the organization as a whole. Effective Performance Management therefore involves sharing an understanding of what needs to be achieved and then managing and developing people in a way that enables such shared objectives to be achieved. A well-developed Performance Management system will include the following:

1. A statement outlining the organization's values and objectives.
2. Individual objectives linked with organizational objectives.
3. Regular performance review throughout the year.
4. Performance related pay.
5. Training and Counseling.

With such system in place it becomes possible to establish Key Results Areas (KRA). Key Result Areas refer to results of an individual which he/she achieve against the expected standards. A reward system can then be tailored to the way in which the individual enables the organization to achieve its results.

Performance Appraisal is a process of systematically evaluating performance of employees and providing feedback on which performance adjustments can be made. Performance Appraisal works on the basis of following formula:

Desired Performance – Actual Performance= Need for Action

To conclude, Performance Management / Performance Appraisal can be regarded as a proactive system of managing employee performance for driving the individuals and the organizations towards desired performance and results. It's about striking a harmonious alignment between individual and organizational objectives for accomplishment of excellence in performance.

3.2 Definitions of Performance Appraisal and Performance Management

According to Edwin B Flippo, "Performance Appraisal is a systematic, periodic and impartial rating of an employee's excellence in matters pertaining to his present job and his potential for future jobs."

According to Dale S. Beach, *"Performance appraisal is systematic evaluation of the individual with respect to his or her performance on the job and his or her potential for development".*

According to Randall S. Schuler, *"Performance appraisal is a formal, structured system of measuring and evaluating an employee's job, related behaviour and outcomes to discover how and why the employee is presently performing on the job and how the employee can perform more effectively in the future so that the employee, organization, and society all benefit."*

According to Dale Yoder, *''Performance appraisal includes all formal procedures used to evaluated personalities and contributions and potentials of group members in a working organisation. It is a continuous process to secure information necessary for making correct and objective decisions on employees."*

According to Gary Desseler, *"Performance Management is a process that consolidates goal settings, performance appraisal and development into single, common systems, the aim of which is to ensure that the employee's performance is supporting the company's strategic aims"*

According to Lockett (1992), *"Performance management aims at developing individuals with the required commitment and competencies for working towards the shared meaningful objectives within an organizational framework"*

3.3 Objectives of Performance Appraisal and Performance Management

The main objectives of Performance Appraisal and Performance Management are discussed below:

1. To enable the employees towards achievement of superior standards of work performance.

2. To help the employees in identifying the knowledge and skills required for performing the job efficiently as this would drive their focus towards performing the right task in the right way.

3. Boosting the performance of the employees by encouraging employee empowerment, motivation and implementation of an effective reward mechanism.

4. Promoting a two way system of communication between the supervisors and the employees for clarifying expectations about the roles and accountabilities, communicating the functional and organizational goals, providing a regular and a transparent feedback for improving employee performance and continuous coaching.

5. Identifying the barriers to effective performance and resolving those barriers through constant monitoring, coaching and development interventions.

6. Creating a basis for several administrative decisions strategic planning, succession planning, promotions and performance based payment.

7. Promoting personal growth and advancement in the career of the employees by helping them in acquiring the desired knowledge and skills.

3.4 Importance of Performance Appraisal and Performance Management

A talented and skilled workforce is the lifeblood of every organization. As the war for talent escalates, companies are quickly learning the importance of having the right people. *"Talent is one of the last frontiers for differentiation. Any company can have a patent or produce a product. The difference is the quality of that product comes with the value of the talent you have."*   *– Elaine Orler, President and Founder of the Talent Function Group*

According to above Quote Talent market is red hot and getting hotter day by day. That's why, keeping in mind the crucial role of your employees and their talent, a recent trend known as **Performance Appraisal and Performance Management** has come into practice.

Widespread attention has been given in recent years to the function of the formal appraisal process because of the idea that a well designed and implemented appraisal system can create many benefits for organizations. ***Mohrman, Resnick-West and Lawler*** found that the appraisal process can:

1. Provide a managerial instrument for goal setting and performance planning with employees,

2. Improve employee motivation and productivity,

3. Encourage interaction concerning employee growth and development,

4. Make available a basis for wage and salary changes, and

5. Generate information for a variety of human resource decisions.

Murphy and Cleveland (1995) defined various ways in which Performance Appraisal/ Performance management can be important to the organizations:

(a) It can improve organizational decisions including rewards allocations, promotions, layoffs and transfers.

(b) It can improve individual career decisions and decisions about where to focus one's time and effort. Individual employees can make many decisions concerning their present and future roles in an organization. They must decide how, or if, they will develop future strengths and what sort of career goals they should pursue.

(c) It can also provide accurate, timely and detailed feedback to assist in the quality of these decisions.

(d) The overall system of Performance Appraisal/ Performance management can assist organizations by providing a set of tools for evaluating the effectiveness of current or planned ways of operating.

(e) Finally, Performance Appraisal/ Performance management can impact employees' views of and commitment to their organization.

The quality of performance appraisal and feedback has a role in the perceptions of the fairness, legitimacy, and rationality of a wide range of organizational practices. It encourages supervisors to observe their employees more closely and to do a better job of managing them. Performance appraisal should be viewed as a beneficial process within the context of an effective system of personnel management. It should be accepted as a normal management responsibility to review the performance of all employees and for all managers to discuss performance with their subordinates on a regular basis for the better of the organization.

3.5 Performance Appraisal Process

Below is the Figure 3.1 which describes the process of Performance Appraisal.

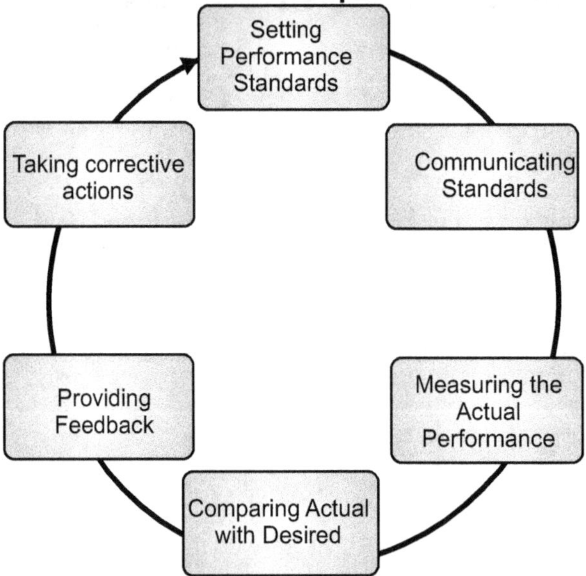

Fig. 3.1: Process of Performance Appraisal

1. **Setting the Performance Standards:** The first step in the process of performance appraisal is setting up of the standards which will be used as a benchmark to compare actual performance of the employees. This step requires setting the performance criteria to judge performance of the employees as successful or unsuccessful of the degrees. To be useful, standards should relate to the desired result of each job. The standards set should be clear, easily understandable and in measurable terms. In case the performance of the employee cannot be measured, great care should be taken to describe the standards.

2. **Communicating the Standards:** There are two parties involved in performance appraisal: appraiser and appraisee. Appraiser is one who does the appraisal and the appraisee is the one whose performance is evaluated. An appraisee should be informed the standards

    This will help them to understand their roles and to know what exactly is expected from them. The standards should also be communicated to the appraisers or the evaluators and if required, the standards can also be modified at this stage itself according to the relevant feedback from the employees or the evaluators.

3. **Measuring the Actual Performance:** The most difficult part of the performance appraisal process is measuring actual performance of the employees i.e. the work done by the employees during a specified period of time. It is a continuous process which involves monitoring the performance throughout the year. This stage requires careful selection of the appropriate techniques of measurement such as personal observation, statistical reports, and written reports for measuring the performance.

4. **Comparing Actual Performance With Desired Performance:** At this stage, actual performance is compared with the desired performance or performance standards. Comparison reveals deviations in the performance of the employees from set standards. This comparison can show actual performance being more than the desired performance, or actual performance being less than the desired performance. It includes recalling, evaluating and analysis of data related to the employees' performance.

5. **Providing Feedback:** Result of the appraisal is communicated and discussed with the employees on one-to-one basis. The focus of this discussion is on communication and listening. The results, problems and possible solutions are discussed, with the aim of problem solving and reaching consensus. The feedback should be given with a positive attitude as this can have an effect on the employees' future performance. The purpose of a meeting should be to solve the problems faced and motivate the employees to perform better.

6. **Taking Corrective Action:** The last step of the process is to take decisions corrective action to overcome the deficiencies or the related HR decisions like rewards, promotions, demotions, transfers etc.

3.6 Performance Appraisal Methods

The decisions regarding the selection of particular type of evaluations usually involves answering questions like what aspects are to be evaluated and how they should be evaluated. Nevertheless the purpose of evaluation is the major guiding factor for such decisions in an organization. For instance Traditional methods like Rating scales, Paired comparison, and other similar methods are appropriate when the purpose of evaluation is identifying suitable employees for promotions and compensations, whereas modern methods are evaluation by employees, peers, customers and self evaluation are more suitable for developing the employees. Thus, managers have to choose carefully from the number of evaluation options available to them.

We shall now see Traditional And Modern Methods of Appraisal with the help of Figure 3.2.

Traditional Methods of Appraisal	Modern Methods of Appraisal
1. Essay Appraisal Method	1. Assessment Centre
2. Grading Method	2. MBO Method
3. Ranking Method	3. Human Resource Accounting Method
4. Checklist Method	4. BARS Method
5. Rating Scales	5. 360 degree Feedback Method
6. Critical Incident Method	6. Computerized and Web based performance appraisal
7. Forced Choice Method	7. Psychological Appraisals
8. Paired Comparison Method	
9. Confidential Report Method	

Fig. 3.2: Traditional and Modern Methods of Appraisal

3.6.1 Traditional Methods of Appraisal

1. **Essay Appraisal Method:** In Essay Appraisal, Appraiser rates the employee in an open-ended manner and put down his impressions about the employee on a continuous basis. These impressions relate to strong and weak points of the employee's behaviour. He takes note of these factors:
    - Job knowledge and skills exhibited by the appraisee while performing his job.

- Appraisee's relationship with the employees and manager.
- Appraisee's personality traits and attitude towards his job, peers, manager and the organization.
- Appraisee's understanding and commitment to organization's goals and objectives.
- Appraisee's potential for organizational future roles.

It is the simplest evaluating method in which evaluator writes an explanation about employee's strength and weakness points, previous performance, positional and suggestions for his (her) performance improvement at the end of evaluation term. This kind of evaluations usually includes some parts of other systems to cause their flexibility. This method often combines with other methods. In essay appraisal, we attempt to focus on behaviours.

2. **Grading Method:** In this technique, the rater considers certain features and marks them according to a scale. The selected features may be analytical ability, cooperativeness, dependability, self-expression, job knowledge, leadership and organizing ability. These may be graded as e.g. A-Outstanding, B-Very good, C-Average, D-Fair, E-Poor and F-Very poor. The actual performance of an employee is then compared with these grades and he is allotted the grade which best describes his performance.

3. **Ranking Method:** Under this method, superior ranks his subordinates in order of their merit, starting from the best to the worst. The relative position of each employee is expressed in terms of his numerical rank. In this type of appraisal, individuals are ranked from highest to lowest. In this method; the manager compares each person with others than work standards.

4. **Checklist Method:** It comprises of series of questions to be responded in "YES" or "NO". Different weightage is assigned to different questions. Some of the questions may be" Does the employee praises his subordinates", "Does the employee shares knowledge with others", "Does the employee takes initiative or volunteer". The weightages are kept confidential with the Human Resource Department. List of positive and negative connotations lead to understanding of the Do's and Don'ts of the job and how one can become more effective. It is time consuming to prepare checklist for different job categories and at times it may mean different things to different managers.

5. **Rating Scales Method:** This is the simplest and the most popular technique for appraising employee performance; the typical rating-scale system consists of several numerical scales, each representing a job-related performance criterion such as dependability, initiative, output, attendance, attitude, co-operation, and the like. Each scale ranges from excellent to poor. The rater checks the appropriate performance level on each criterion, and then computes the employee's total

numerical score. The number of points scored may be linked to salary increases, whereby so many points equal a rise of some percentage. Rating scales offer the advantages of adaptability, relatively easy use and low cost. Nearly every type of job can be evaluated in a short time, and rater does not need any training to use the scale. The disadvantages of this method are several. The rater's biases are likely to influence evaluation, and the biases are particularly pronounced on 71 subjective criteria such as cooperation, attitude and initiative. Furthermore, numerical scoring gives an illusion of precision that is really unfounded.

6. **Critical Incident Method**: In the Critical Incident Method, the Manager has to keep a written record of initial incidents. It would have both good and bad incidents of the job performance and behaviour. Such individuals are rated over a time period after which evaluation and feedback is provided. Recordings of the incidents help in stating the facts, while evaluating helps in giving specific feedback. But this is time consuming. In fact it is difficult to define the "Critical" Incidents and it may lead to friction as an employee may think that the manager is keeping close watch on them.

7. **Forced Choice Method:** In this, the Rater is given a series of statements about an employee. These statements are arranged in blocks of 2 or more, and the rater indicates which statement is most or least descriptive of the employee. Typical statements are:

    1. Learns fast _ _ _ _ _ _ _ _ _ _ _ _ _ _ _ _ _ _ _ works hard
    2. Work is reliable_ _ _ _ _ _ _ _ _ _ _ _ _ _ _ _ _ performance is a good example for
    3. Absents often_ _ _ _ _ _ _ _ _ _ _ _ _ _ _ _ _ _ others usually tardy.

    As in the checklist method, the Rater is simply expected to select the statements that describe the rate. Actual assessment is done by the HR Department. This approach is known as the forced choice method because the Rater is forced to select statements, which are readymade. The advantage of this method is the absence of personal bias in rating. The disadvantage is that the statements may not be properly framed – they may not be precisely descriptive of the Ratee's traits.

8. **Paired Comparison Method:** In this method, the appraiser compares each employee with all others in a group one at a time. After all the comparisons, on the basis of the overall comparisons, the employees are given the final rankings. Under this method, the appraiser compares each employee with every other employee one at a time. For example there are five employees named A, B, C, D and E. The performance of A is first compared with the performance of B and a decision is made about whose performance is better. Then A is compared with C, D and E in that order. The same procedure is repeated for other employees. The number of comparisons may be calculated with the help of a formula which reads thus:

N (N-1)/ 2 where N stands for the number of employees to be compared. If there are 10 employees, the number of comparisons will be 10(10 − 1)/2 = 45. After the completion of comparison, the results can be tabulated and a rank is created from the number of times each person is considered to be superior.

9. **Confidential Report Method:** It is mostly used in government departments. This report is prepared at the end of a year. It shall have certain items like attendance, leadership, initiative, ability to work with others, job knowledge, integrity etc. The superior records his impression about the 74 subordinate considering these items. This system does not offer any feedback to the subordinates hence there is no surety of why he/ she is rated low than the others

3.6.2 Modern Methods of Appraisal

1. **Assessment Centre:** An assessment center typically involves the use of methods like social/informal events, tests and exercises, assignments being given to a group of employees to assess their competencies to take higher responsibilities in the future. Generally, employees are given an assignment similar to the job they would be expected to perform if promoted.

   This review of potential is concerned with forecasting the direction in which an individual's career should go and the rate at which he is expected to develop. The trained evaluators observe and evaluate employees as they perform the assigned jobs and are evaluated on job related characteristics.

   The major competencies that are judged in assessment centers are interpersonal skills, intellectual capability, planning and organizing capabilities, motivation, career orientation etc. Assessment centers are also an effective way to determine the training and development needs of the targeted employees.

2. **Management by Objectives (MBO):** It is also called as "Goal Setting Method". MBO (or Management By Objectives) is a technique credited to *Management Guru Peter Drucker*, to describe a method of performance management that is based on the setting of clear and measurable objectives, and the use of those objectives to evaluate and review performance. When done correctly, MBO is probably the best and fairest way to plan for and create effectively performing employees.

   The principle behind Management by Objectives (MBO) is to make sure that everybody within the organization has a clear understanding of the aims, or objectives, of that organization, as well as awareness of their own roles and responsibilities in achieving those aims. The complete MBO system is to get managers and empowered employees acting to implement and achieve their plans, which automatically achieve those of the organization.

MBO Strategy: Three Basic Parts:

All individuals within an organization are assigned a special set of objectives that they try to reach during a normal operating period. These objectives are mutually set and agreed upon by individuals and their managers. Performance reviews are conducted periodically to determine how close individuals are to attaining their objectives. Rewards are given to individuals on the basis of how close they come to reaching their goals.

MBO as a goal setting and appraisal programme consists of six steps:

- o **Setting organizational goals:** Based on firm's strategic plan establish organizational plan for next year, and from this set company's goals.
- o **Set departmental goals:** Departmental heads take these company goals and with their superiors jointly set goals for their departments.
- o **Discuss departmental goals:** Departmental heads discuss departmental goals with their subordinates. They ask the subordinates to set their individual goals.
- o **Define expected results:** Departmental heads and their subordinates set short term individual performance targets.
- o **Performance reviews:** Departmental heads compare each employee's actual and targeted performance.
- o **Provide feedback:** Departmental heads and employee discuss and evaluate the latter's' progress.

3. **Human Resource Accounting Method:** Human resources are valuable assets for every organization. Human resource accounting method tries to find the relative worth of these assets in the terms of money. In this method the performance appraisal of the employees is judged in terms of cost and contribution of the employees. The cost of employees include all the expenses incurred on them like their compensation, recruitment and selection costs, induction and training costs etc whereas their contribution includes the total value added (in monetary terms). The difference between the cost and the contribution will be the performance of the employees. Ideally, the contribution of the employees should be greater than the cost incurred on them.

4. **BARS Method (Behaviourally Anchored Rating Scales):** This method is combination of the rating scale and critical incident techniques of performance appraisal. It is a tool that anchors a numerical rating scale with specific behavioural examples of good or poor performance.

   Behaviourally Anchored Scales, sometimes called behavioural expectation scales, are rating scales whose scale points are determined by statements of effective and ineffective behaviours. They are said to be behaviourally anchored in that the scales represent a range of descriptive statements of behaviour varying from the least to the most effective. A rater must indicate which behaviour on each scale best describes an employee's performance.

Behaviourally anchored rating scales (BARS) have the following features:

- o   Areas of performance to be evaluated are identified and defined by people who will use the scales.
- o   The scales are anchored by descriptions of actual job behaviour that, supervisors agree, represent specific levels of performance. The result is a set of rating scales in which both dimensions and anchors are precisely defined.
- o   All dimensions of performance to be evaluated are based on observable behaviours and are relevant to the job being evaluated since BARS are tailor-made for the job.
- o   Since the raters who will actually use the scales are actively involved in the development process.

They are more likely to be committed to the final product. BARS were developed to provide results which subordinates could use to improve performance. Superiors would feel comfortable to give feedback to the rates. Further, BARS help overcome rating errors. Unfortunately, this method too suffers from distortion inherent in most rating techniques.

BARS have Five Stages:

(1)   Generate critical incidents.

(2)   Develop performance dimensions.

(3)   Relocate incidents.

(4)   Rating of level of performance for each incident and

(5)   Development of the final instrument.

5. **360 degree Feedback Method:** 360 degree feedback is also known as 'multi-source feedback. First developed at General Electric, US in 1992, the system has become popular in our country too. It is the latest method and for some people, it is the most exciting development in the field of performance appraisal. It is systematic collection and feedback of performance data on an individual or group derived from number of stakeholders. The data is feedback in the form of ratings against various performance dimensions. The feedback is taken from the person they report to, the peers and the other team members of other parts of the organization with whom one deals with. Self-Assessment is also a part of the process. The range of the feedback could be extended to include other stakeholders- external customers, clients or suppliers. This is sometimes known as 540 degree feedback. The feedback may also be in form of 180 degree or upward feedback which is generated by subordinates to their managers.

360 degree feedback broadens the perspective of how an employee is perceived by others, encourages openness, gains acceptance and is more reliable because of multi-rating. It increases awareness and relevance of competencies, awareness of developmental needs and reinforces the desired competencies of the business. It helps in identifying the key developmental needs of individual, department and organization as a whole alongwith strengths that can be used to the advantage of business. It develops a climate which is supportive of continuous improvements and raises self-awareness of people about how they personally affect others- positively and negatively.

It provides the clear picture to the senior management of a given individual; perception of feedback is more valid and objective, leading to acceptance of results and actions required. But at times people may not give honest feedback. People are being put under pressure of receiving or giving feedback. This is over reliance on technology and too much bureaucracy. There is lack of action following feedback. However these can be minimized by careful designing, communication, training, and follow up. 21% of US organizations are using 360 degree feedback programs. In India it is used in Dr. Reddy Laboratories, NIIT, Satyam, Infosys, Philips India and many more.

6. **Computerized and Web based Performance Appraisal:** Nowadays, several performance appraisal software programmes are available. These software programmes enable managers to keep computerized notes on subordinates during the year, and then to combine these with ratings of employees on several performance traits. The software programmes then generate written text to support each part of the appraisal. In the traditional Appraisal system, the paper based appraisal causes a lot of manual work, which is time consuming, not secure and difficult to analyze the performance. Whereas Web based performance appraisal provides an easy way to conduct appraisal.

7. **Psychological Appraisals:** Large organization employs full-time industrial psychologists. These psychologists are used for evaluations. They assess an individual's future potential and past performance. The appraisal normally consists of in-depth interviews, psychological tests, discussions with supervisors and a review' of other evaluations. The psychologists then write an evaluation of the employee's intellectual, emotional, motivational and other-related characteristics that suggest individual potential and may predict future performance. The evaluation by the psychologist may be for a specific job opening for which the person is being considered. Or it may be a global assessment of his or her future potential. From these evaluations, placement and development decisions may be made to shape the person's career.

3.7 Purpose of Performance Appraisal

The major purpose of performance appraisal is to evaluate how well employees have conducted their duty. Performance appraisal helps to keep a record of each employee's job performance, including what efforts they have made and what have they achieved. Evaluation differentiates employees on the basis of their job performance, alongwith other factors like personality, behaviour, etc. The purpose of Performance Appraisal is as follows:

1. **Provide Continuous Feedback:** It is essential for the employers to know what performance and achievements have been made by their employees. But, it is also equally important for an employee to know where they stand, where they are going and how they are going to get there. Thus, giving feedback to employees is also a major purpose of performance appraisal.

2. **Measure Performance Accurately:** Every company has to set mutually acceptable criteria or performance standards so that it could with the employee performance which will directly help in accurate measurement of employee's job performance. In fact it is necessary for the company to know where it is heading and in which direction.

3. **Provides Clarity of Expectation and Actual Results:** Every employee of the organization should be communicated about their duties and also about the expectations of organization from them. They should also be told how well they have done their duties and how can they improve their performance in future work. They should be made clear about how near they are to do their expectation.

4. **Identify areas of Weakness of Employees:** All employees cannot be all-rounder. Some of the employees have their weak points which if not sorted at right time can prove as liability to the organization. Performance appraisal helps in identifying such weak points.

5. **Determining Training and Developmental Needs:** Determining weak points is not enough but at the same time company should make efforts to eliminate them. A properly carried out performance appraisal is a tool to determine what necessary steps are to be taken in order to help the employees in improving their performance. The increment in skills and knowledge develop an overall personality, attitude and behaviour of the employees.

6. **Provide Career Path:** Performance appraisal works as a mirror to employees and it clearly shows what they are professionally and where they stand. On the other hand, it helps the company in recognizing employees with potential. Companies provide career development opportunities to such employees and pave their way to a successful and stable career.

7. **Determine Promotion of Employees:** Performance appraisal helps in charting progress of employees. Such charts can be used by the employers to determine whether or not to promote their employees. They also help in identifying the employees who most deserves to be promoted.

8. **Taking Corrective Actions:** Performance appraisal distinguishes excellent and poor performing employees. Results of performance appraisal help the employers in taking corrective actions. Such actions may be counseling or warning the poor performers to improve performance and to prevent the occurrence of undesirable results.

9. **Decide Termination and Retention of Employees:** Progress report of employees does not only help in determining promotion but also in determining termination. Employees, with poor reports, are at first consulted with proper direction. But, if the supervisors don't find any growth after consultation, they will be forced to take severe action like termination.

10. **Evaluate Effectiveness of HRM Functions:** Recruitment, selection, employee training, rewarding, etc. are some functions of human resource management whose effectiveness can only be analyzed when the performance of employees are appraised.

11. **Decide Salary and Rewards:** Performance appraisal of employees helps the supervisors in knowing their job performance and the right amount to pay them. The employees will receive wages as per the contribution they have made. The impressive contributors are also rewarded by the company as per the organization's policy.

12. **Reduces Grievances:** Grievances may occur in the company when employees feel unfairly treated or biased. *For an instance, an employee might feel that his co-worker is being paid more by the company even though both of them are posted at the same job level.* During such situation, employers can use the reports of performance appraisal to clarify the employees that they are being paid on the basis of their job performance, rather than the position they hold.

13. **Openness in Communication:** The complete process of performance appraisal includes continuous feedback from the supervisors. This way, performance appraisal works as a bridge of communication between the employers and employees. Also, open communication helps in strengthening the employer-employee relationship or superior-subordinate relationship.

14. **Motivate Performance:** When performances of employees are timely appraised, they are motivated to make the superior performance. It is because of the fact that

   - They want to enjoy the perk of being an excellent employee or
   - They fear negative reactions from the supervisors.

When employees know that they are heading in right direction, it develops a sense of satisfaction in them.

15. **Improves Decision Making Ability:** It becomes easier for the organization to take right decision when performance appraisal works as a helping hand to the company in making the complete statistical data available.

3.8 Why to Measure Performance ?

It is generally said that Performance Appraisal can have positive impact on organizations. They help to improve organizational effectiveness, particularly when attributes are linked with organizational objectives. Measuring and managing employee performance is important because it gives you the ability to properly gauge worker efficiency, identify who is working hard and who isn't, determine how to properly compensate your workforce, and improve your workplace's overall productivity. Measuring the performance of an employee is a key strategy for organizational success.

Appraisals can helps to reduce employee's uncertainty while promoting more effective communication between supervisors and subordinates. Communication received through appraisal feedback is essential for encouraging employees to continue on positive path or to guide the employees in improving problem areas. It helps to promote trust among the organizational members which affects the performance positively. If appraisals are well structured and applied it can help to minimize distractions in the organizations and can promote trust within the organization.

Clarity of goals and desired performance helps to reduced uncertainty about job related expectations. It actually creates a forum for collaboration in ascertaining goals. This in fact leads to greater acceptance and satisfaction with appraisal results.

Measurement of performance helps employees to understand how well their job goals are met with organizational goals. Thus measuring and managing performance helps businesses as well as the employees to better understand their peers, organization's revealing the high achievers and highlighting any issues.

3.9 Performance Appraisal v/s Performance Management

Performance Appraisal	Performance Management
1. An organized way of evaluating the performance and potential of employees for their future growth and development is known as Performance Appraisal.	1. The Complete process of managing the human resources of the organization is known as Performance Management.
2. Performance Appraisal is a system.	2. Performance Management is the process.

Performance Appraisal	Performance Management
3. Performance Appraisal is Inflexible	3. Performance Management is Flexible.
4. Performance Appraisal is an Operational tool to improve the efficiency of employees	4. Performance Management is a Strategic Tool.
5. Performance Appraisal is conducted by a Human resources department of the organization.	5. Managers are held responsible for Performance Management
6. In Performance Appraisal corrections are made retrospectively	6. Performance Management is forward looking
7. Performance Appraisal has an Individualistic approach	7. Performance Management is Collectivism approach
8. Performance Appraisal is carried on an eventual basis	8. Performance Management is ongoing process.

Therefore, we can say that the term performance appraisal and performance management are completely different. But, it can't be said that they are contradictory because performance appraisal itself is a part of performance management.

3.10 Potential Management

First we should know the meaning of Potential. "Potential "means inherent capacity for coming into being. The dictionary meaning of potential takes into account latent energy. By using their potential, human beings are capable of "Taking Charge of Them". According to The Concise Oxford Dictionary (1982), the term "Potential" means "capable of coming into being or action.

The term "Potential" is typically used to suggest that an individual has the qualities (e.g. characteristics, motivation, skills, abilities, experiences etc.) to effectively perform and contribute in broader or different roles in the organization, at some point in the future. Potential is associated with possibilities for the future rather than with problems in current performance.

Some employees are more talented than others due to which other managers and executives generally have disputes. The more debatable point is how to treat the people who appear to have the highest potential. In an organization all employees are talented in some way and, therefore, all should receive equal opportunities for growth. The process of assessing the potential in employees deals with the question of whether they will be able to manage positions in future which involves responsibilities and different challenges. As long as individuals are being able to handle such responsibilities and challenges they are being able to have Potential. Competencies of an employee to perform well in the current job are not automatic indicators of his potential for promotion or other purposes. People may not have potential of equal degree. Potentiality differs from persons to persons. Some people may have high potential, some may have less. It is the potential appraisal that assesses degree of potential people does have.

There exist some indicators of potential which managers meticulously observe and consider while making decisions about their potential. Some of the indicators are a sense of reality, imagination, power of analysis, breadth of vision, and persuasiveness.

1. **Sense of Reality:** People usually act based on their thought process. A sense of reality refers to the extent to which a person thinks and acts objectively, controls his emotional pressure, and continues to pursue realistic projects with enthusiasm and achieves business goals.

2. **Imagination:** Imagination is the mind's eye. A man dreams by virtue of his imaginative power. It is the ability to let the mind range over a wide variety of possible causes of actions to achieve specific results. Imagination goes beyond conventional approaches to situations and does not remain confined to, 'this work is done in only one way'.

3. **Power of Analysis:** Power of analysis refers to the capacity to reformulate, innovate, break down, and transform an apparently complicated situation into manageable terms. People with power of analysis believe in, 'innovate or evaporate'.

4. **Breadth of Vision:** People need visionary skills and their breadth of vision should be wider. Breadth of vision means the ability to examine a problem in the context of a much broader framework of reference. People with breadth of vision can detect relationships with those aspects within a specific situation which could impact the situation.

5. **Persuasiveness:** Persuasiveness helps one trying as long as it takes to produce results. It is the ability to sell ideas to others and gain a continuing commitment. Using managerial authority may not always produce results. Persuasion refers to using personal influence by way of negotiation.These five indicators are standard factors that are considered while judging the potential of any individual. These have helped many organizations in taking decisions.

Objectives of Potential Management:

1. **Identification of Employees Having Capabilities to Perform Higher Level Jobs:** It identifies people who have potential to take over higher jobs. This task is difficult

to accomplish in industrial settings. It may take the help of assessment centre/ development centres to find out suitable/capable employees for promotion.

2. **Assessment of General Potential:** It assesses whether the employees have abilities to perform some types of work. Employees' aptitudes, level of competency, skill are appraised for better utilization in the organization activities.

3. **Identification of Training Needs of Employees:** For growth and development of organization employees' development of skill, knowledge, abilities is needed. This is possible through training. Potential appraisal identifies the area which requires training for reinforcement/improvement.

4. **Implementing Succession Planning Activities:** It helps organization to effectively carry out succession planning activities by way of providing data / information in respect of employees who are suitable for filling in vacant posts.

5. **Assisting Employees in Personal Development Process:** It makes the employees aware of their strengths and weaknesses through feedback / counseling, discussion programmes so that they can prepare their personal development plan effectively.

6. **Helping Organization to Decide its Strategy:** It makes organization know its competent, effective, potential workforce as also non-achievers, dead woods, non-performers. Looking into strength of human resources, organization can decide its strategy. For example, the organization can decide whether it can go for business process reengineering, diversification of activities, reduction of employees through VRS etc.

7. **Helping Organization to Survive, Grow and Develop:** In the changing scenario, every organization has to face tough competition against MNCs and other organizations. For confrontation against such challenges and for sustenance, growth, development of organization, it needs dynamic workforce. Potential appraisal helps organization to develop the employees and to create a reservoir of committed, competent workforce who can give befitting challenges through production of quality goods and service at low rate.

Training and Development - A Conceptual Framework

Pragmatic Insight: Reliance Industries Limited is one of the largest private sector companies in India with a 24,000 strong workforce. This fortune 500 company has won several awards for its training policies and programmes. The company believes in people empowerment through five scalable approaches i.e. greater knowledge, opportunity, responsibility, accountability and reward.

The main objective of Reliance Industries Limited in terms of Training and development is to groom people both in personal and professional capabilities. The company believes in achieving competitive advantage through consistently efficient human capital. It has wide range of varied customized training programmes to cater the specific needs of the workforce and meet its strategic goals. For instance it has several target oriented training programmes for its employees like competency development and soft skills learning. It has conducts 360 other programmes to meet the diverse skills needs of employees. One such unique training programme for employees who are newly recruited is called "Dronacharya Scheme." Under this programme, Senior Personnel (*Dronacharyas*) take charge of two to three new employees (*the Arjunas*) and train them intensively for independent positions in three to six months. Through its different training programmes the company seeks to develop competitive advantages through its human capital.

The above example of Reliance Industries Limited showcases the significance of training programmes in the accomplishment of the corporate goals. We shall now discuss the relevant aspects of employee training in this chapter.

3.11 Introduction to Training and Development

Let's start with Quote,"

Tell me and I forget, Teach me and I remember, involve me and I learn- Benjamin Franklin.

The essence of teaching is to make learning contagious, to have one idea spark another. Marva Collins

As rightly said, Training is a continuous learning process. It is value addition activity undertaken by an organization to enrich the value of its core assets, namely its people. It plays a vital role in enhancing the efficiency, productivity and performance of the employees. It is learning process that helps employees to acquire new knowledge and the skills required to perform their present jobs efficiently. Rapid technological developments and the changes in production process have forced the management of various companies to treat training as continuous process of the organization. In fact the strategic goals of organization usually form the basis for its training programmes.

Training typically comprises of predetermined programmes to achieve the desired performance efficiency at various levels- individual, group and organizational. In simple terms, Training is all about making a difference between where the worker stands at present and where he will be after some point of time.

Training is short term skill development exercise meant for non-managerial employees either to learn a job or to overcome their deficiency in the performance of the present job. The success of any training programmes lies in recognizing training needs within the organization and then designing and implementing training programmes based on those needs in order to carry out a continuous up gradation of knowledge, skills and employee attitudes. In fact a sustained training effort by an organization usually leads to creation of a highly competent and motivated workforce that is all set to take on the challenges of performance and productivity. To sum up we can say, Training is the process by which an employee acquires the necessary knowledge and skills to perform the job. On the other hand, **Development** is related to enhancing the conceptual skills of the employee, which helps individual towards achieving maturity and self-actualization. Development refers to the overall holistic and educational growth and maturity of people in managerial positions. The process of development is related with insights, attitudes, adaptability, leadership and human relations. Development of an employee is wider term. It is continuous process. Training is the part of this process. Thus, Training is the part of ongoing Employee Development Programme.

3.12 Definitions of Training and Development

- ***According to Dale S. Beach*** defines Training as 'the organized procedure by which people learn knowledge and/or skill for a definite purpose'.
- ***According to Edwin Flippo***, 'Training is the act of increasing the skills of an employee for doing a particular job'.
- ***According to Gary Dessler,*** Training refers to the "methods used to give new or present employees the skills they needed to perform their jobs".
- ***According to Michael J Jucius,*** "Training is any process by which the attitudes, skills and abilities of the employees to perform specific jobs are improved".
- ***In the words of Michael Armstrong***, "Employee development, often referred to as Human Resource Development (HRD) is about the provision of learning, development and training opportunities in order to improve individual, team and organizational performance.
- ***According to C. B. Memoria***, "Development covers not only activities, which improve job performance, but also those, which bring about growth of personalities, help individuals in the progress towards maturity and actualization of their potential capacities so that they become not only good employee but better men and women.

3.13 Objectives of Training and Development

The objectives of training and development are not limited to just increasing productivity and efficiency, but the busy market and ceaselessly active competition of today, demands much more than that from organizations. It focuses on addition of new skills and improvement of the existing skill-set, which is an extremely important aspect of a business. Following are the Objectives of Training and Development:

1. **To Enhance Knowledge of Employees:** Organizations' need to help their employees to keep up their knowledge in tune with the contemporary trends. Due to advancement and innovations in science and technology, organizations' should support their personnel in the battle against obsolescence. Personnel are to be exposed to refresher courses and developmental programmes with a view to improve their utility to the organization.

2. **To Improve Job Related Skills:** Some employees are not able to perform their jobs well. They possess inadequate skills and knowledge of their assignments with the result that they produce poor quality and volume of output, waste resources, damage equipment and tools, respond insufficiently to the supervisor's instructions and so on. They should provide with a training course for the purpose of removing their deficiencies and fitting them to their jobs in order to enhance their efficiency.

3. **To Develop Proper Job-Related Attitudes:** The employees have to be trained to develop positive and helpful attitudes towards their jobs, superiors, colleagues and juniors, the goals, policies and procedures of the organization and to the environment of the work place. Employees sometimes tend to be ignorant, indifferent and even hostile towards their jobs in their inter-personnel relations and to the work culture. Attitude development and socialization of the personnel is essential for generating teamwork, ensuring discipline and maintaining consistent behaviour.

4. **To Prepare for Higher Responsibilities:** The personnel need to have opportunities for advancement in their careers. Concurrently, they should also be striving for assuming higher responsibilities and performing more complex tasks with competence. For this purpose, an organization may design a system whereby opportunities are made available to personnel for their career advancement and simultaneously preparing them through training for higher positions.

5. **To Facilitate Organizational Changes:** Organizations' need to be dynamic to cope with, adjust and adapt to the changes in technology and other environmental forces. The personnel have to be conditioned to learn new skills and capabilities to enable them to be receptive to required changes and to assimilate them. For this purpose, they are to be properly trained. Training of personnel is one of the approaches for the organization to win over their resistance to change which is caused by fear, anxiety and unfamiliarity.

3.14 Scope of Training and Development

The Scope of training depends upon the categories of employees to be trained. As we all know that training is a continuous process and not only needed for the newly selected personnel but also for the existing personnel at all levels of the organization. The scope of training is wide.

The essential elements in any enterprise are materials, equipment and human resource. Training, allied to the other human resource specializations within management, ensures a pool of manpower of the required levels of expertise at the right time. One of the most important factors in this regard is the view of training and trainers. They are seen as an expense, a service, as second rate to production or as a necessary evil. Training has tended to fall behind other management activities, especially in the planning phase. It is often carried out as a reaction to immediate needs, a patch up operation in many cases, instead of an ordered activity. If the organizations accept the fact that people are greatest asset, then it is easy to convince the top management that training is a principal management function. It is an act of faith to pass on one's knowledge, skills and attitudes to those who follow. It basically creates a climate in which learning is seen to be an important part of work. Scope of the Training enhances job related performance, organizational effectiveness, makes behavioural changes and develops life skills leading to personal growth of employees. It equips an individual with competencies that helps him/her to cope up with day-to-day problems of living and manage interpersonal relations and improves them. Ultimately it aims to commitment to profession through better Quality work life and employee development.

3.15 Benefits of Training

Benefits of training and development to the Organization are as under:

Benefits of Training in Organization:

- Training improves the quantity and quality of the workforce. It increases the skills and knowledge base of the employees.
- It improves upon the time and money required to reach the company's goals. *For example: Trained salesmen achieve and exceed their targets faster than inexperienced and untrained salesmen.*
- Training helps to identify the highly skilled and talented employees and the company can give those jobs higher responsibilities.
- Trained employees are highly efficient in comparison to untrained ones.
- Reduces the need to constantly supervise and overlook the employees.
- Improves job satisfaction and thus boosts morale.

Benefits of Development in Organization:

- Exposes executives to the latest techniques and trends in their professional fields.
- Ensures that the company has an adequate number of managers with knowledge and skill at any given point.
- Helps in the long-term growth and survival of the company.
- Creates an effective team of managers who can handle the company issues without fail.
- Ensures that the employees utilize their managerial and leadership skills in particular to the fullest

3.16 Role of Training in Organizations

In Today's dynamic business environment, job knowledge and skills to handle the continuously changing job contents need continuous up gradation. For this Training has to be imparted continuously. It also becomes imperative to handle diverse situations and to deal with varied clients, customers, vendors, suppliers, colleagues and business partners. Training deals with developing people attitudes which help the individuals to deal with different situations and people according to one's advantage. In light of these diverse factors, Training has become extremely important for organizations in maintaining its human resources at their peak performance levels. The challenge for the organization therefore is to introduce a range of new innovative training and development programmes. Training is the most important technique of human resource development. No organization can get a candidate who exactly matches with the job and the organizational requirements. Hence training is important to develop the employee and make him suitable for the job. Training and development programmes are the corner stone of sound management, for it makes employees more effective and productive. When carried out properly, training enables both people and organization to create more opportunities in future. Following aspects will helps us to identify the role of training in organizations:

1. **Optimum Development of Human Resource:** Training and development helps to provide an opportunity for the development of technical and behavioural skills of human resources in an organization. It also helps an employee in attaining personal growth. Providing training to the human resources not only increases the skill, knowledge and talent in them but also they can make themselves capable of occupying positions at higher levels.

2. **Enhanced Utilization of Human Resources:** Training and development helps in optimizing the utilization of human resource that further helps the employee to achieve harmony between the organizational goals as well as their individual goals.

3. **Development of Skills:** Training and development helps in increasing the job knowledge and skills of employee at each level. It helps to expand the horizons of human intellect and an overall personality of the employees. Training increases the skills of employees and they perform the job better than before.

4. **Increases Productivity:** Training and development helps in increasing productivity of the employees. Increase in performance and productivity are most evident on the part of employee who are not yet fully aware of the most efficient and effective ways of performing their jobs .

5. **Creates Team Spirit:** Training and development helps in developing the sense of team work, team spirit, and inter-team collaborations. It helps in including the zeal

to learn within the employees. Team learning is a process of aligning and developing the capacity of a team to create the results its members truly desires.

6. **Improves Organizational Culture:** Training and development helps to develop and improve the organizational health, culture and effectiveness and it also helps in creating a learning culture within the organization.

7. **Improves Organizational Climate:** Training and development helps in building positive perception and feeling about the organization. The employees get these feelings from leaders, subordinates and peers.

8. **Improves Quality of Work and Life:** Training and development helps in improving quality of work and life.

9. **Creates Healthy Work Environment:** Training and development helps in creating healthy working environment and it also helps to build good employee relationships so that individual goals can be align with organizational goals.

10. **Increases Morale and Loyalty:** Training and development helps in improving the morale and loyalty of the work force. A trained worker's morale increases because of the support and encouragement he gets from seniors at work place.

It is an established fact that human resources are assets and strategic business tools in an organization to drive corporate performance that provides a distinct competitive advantage. So Motivation is a tonic for the workers. The more you motivate your subordinate, the more productive they become in their work. Work becomes enjoyable, challenging for them through motivation. To conclude the role of training programmes in an organization are seemed to be vehicle which takes personnel from one place to another.

3.17 Types of Training

A multitude of methods of training are used to train employees. Training methods are categorized into two groups:

- **On the Job methods:** It refers to the methods that are applied at the workplace, while the employee is actually working.

- **Off the Job methods:** It refers to the methods that are used away from workplaces.

Training methods represent the medium to impart skills and knowledge to employees. Management development is a systematic process of growth and development by which the managers develop their abilities to manage. It is concerned with not only improving the performance of managers but also giving them opportunities for growth and development. Managers can improve their knowledge and skills through formal training and also through on the job experiences. It is said that "Learning becomes fruitful only when theory is combined with practice" and hence through training methods organization can make learning fruitful.

On the Job Methods	Off the Job Methods
Job Rotation	Lectures and Conferences
Coaching	Vestibule Training
Mentoring	Simulation Exercises
Job Instruction Technology	Sensitivity Training
Apprenticeship	Transactional Training
Understudy	–

3.17.1 On the Job Training Methods

Under these methods new or inexperienced employees learn through observing peers or managers performing the job and trying to imitate their behaviour. These methods do not cost much and are less disruptive as employees are always on the job, training is given on the same machines and experience would be on already approved standards, and above all the trainee is learning while earning. Some of the commonly used methods are:

- **Job Rotation:** It is the process of training employees by rotating them through a series of related jobs. Rotation not only makes a person well acquainted with different jobs, but it also lightens boredom and allows to develop rapport with a number of people. Job Rotation must be logical.

- **Coaching:** Coaching is a one-to-one training. It helps in quickly identifying the weak areas and tries to focus on them. It also offers the benefit of transferring theory learning into practice. The biggest problem is that it perpetrates the existing practices and styles. In India most of the scooter mechanics are trained only through this method.

- **Mentoring:** The focus in this training is on the development of attitude. It is used for managerial employees. Mentoring is always done by a senior inside person. It is also one-to- one interaction, like coaching.

- **Job Instructional Technique (JIT):** There are various steps to accomplish a particular task. In this method of training, a worker is guided by a supervisor or a trainer who tells him/her about the exact steps for the accomplishment of the work. Moreover, new works are being taught to the workers by the supervisor. It is a Step by step (structured) on the job training method in which a suitable trainer:
  - Prepares a trainee with an overview of the job, its purpose, and the results desired,
  - Demonstrates the task or the skill to the trainee,
  - Allows the trainee to show the demonstration on his or her own, and
  - Follows up to provide feedback and help.

It helps us:

1.   To deliver step-by-step instruction.

2.   To know when the learner has learned.

3.   To be due diligent (in many work-place environments).

- **Apprenticeship:** Apprenticeship is a system of training a new generation of practitioners of a skill. This method of training is in vogue in those trades, crafts and technical fields in which a long period is required for gaining proficiency. The trainees serve as apprentices to experts for long periods. They have to work in direct association with and also under the direct supervision of their masters. The object of such training is to make the trainees all-round craftsmen. It is an expensive method of training. Also, there is no guarantee that the trained worker will continue to work in the same organization after securing training. The apprentices are paid remuneration according the apprenticeship agreements.

- **Understudy:** In this method, a superior gives training to a subordinate as his understudy like an assistant to a manager or director (in a film). The subordinate learns through experience and observation by participating in handling day to day problems. Basic purpose is to prepare subordinate for assuming the full responsibilities and duties.

3.17.2 Off the Job Training Methods

Off-the-job training methods are conducted in separate from the job environment, study material is supplied, there is full concentration on learning rather than performing, and there is freedom of expression. Important methods include:

- **Lectures and Conferences:** Lectures and conferences are the traditional and direct method of instruction. Every training programme starts with lecture and conference. It's a verbal presentation for a large audience. However, the lectures have to be motivating and creating interest among trainees. The speaker must have considerable depth in the subject. In the colleges and universities, lectures and seminars are the most common methods used for training.

- **Vestibule Training:** Vestibule Training is a term for near-the-job training, as it offers access to something new (learning). In vestibule training, the workers are trained in a prototype environment on specific jobs in a special part of the plant. An attempt is made to create working condition similar to the actual workshop conditions. After training workers in such condition, the trained workers may be put on similar jobs in the actual workshop. This enables the workers to secure training in the best methods to work and to get rid of initial nervousness. During the Second

World War II, this method was used to train a large number of workers in a short period of time. It may also be used as a preliminary to on-the job training. Duration ranges from few days to few weeks. It prevents trainees to commit costly mistakes on the actual machines.

- **Simulation Exercises**: Simulation is any artificial environment exactly similar to the actual situation. There are four basic simulation techniques used for imparting training:

  A. Management Games,

  B. Case Study,

  C. Role Playing, And

  D. In-Basket Training.

A. Management Games: Properly designed games help to ingrain thinking habits, analytical, logical and reasoning capabilities, importance of team work, time management, to make decisions lacking complete information, communication and leadership capabilities. Use of management games can encourage novel, innovative mechanisms for coping with stress. Management games orient a candidate with practical applicability of the subject. These games help to appreciate management concepts in a practical way. Different games are used for training general managers and the middle management and functional heads – executive Games and functional heads.

B. Case Study: Case studies are complex examples which give an insight into the context of a problem as well as illustrating the main point. Case Studies are trainee centered activities based on topics that demonstrate theoretical concepts in an applied setting. A case study allows the application of theoretical concepts to be demonstrated, thus bridging the gap between theory and practice, encourage active learning, provides an opportunity for the development of key skills such as communication, group working and problem solving, and increases the trainees" enjoyment of the topic and hence their desire to learn.

C. Role Playing: Each trainee takes the role of a person affected by an issue and studies the impacts of the issues on human life and/or the effects of human activities on the world around us from the perspective of that person. It emphasizes the "real- world" side of science and challenges students to deal with complex problems with no single "right" answer and to use a variety of skills beyond those employed in a typical research project. In particular, role-playing presents the student a valuable opportunity to learn not just the course content, but other perspectives on it. The steps involved in role playing include defining objectives, choose context and roles, introducing the exercise, trainee preparation/research, the role-play, concluding discussion, and assessment. Types of role play may be multiple role play, single role play, role rotation, and spontaneous role play etc.

D. In-basket training: In-basket exercise, also known as in-tray training, consists of a set of business papers which may include e-mail SMSs, reports, memos, and other items. Now the trainer is asked to prioritize the decisions to be made immediately and the ones that can be delayed.

- **Sensitivity Training:** Sensitivity training is also known as laboratory or T-group training. This training is about making people understand about themselves and others reasonably, which is done by developing in them social sensitivity and behavioural flexibility. It is ability of an individual to sense what others feel and think from their own point of view. It reveals information about his or her own personal qualities, concerns, emotional issues, and things that he or she has in common with other members of the group. It is the ability to behave suitably in light of understanding.

A group's trainer refrains from acting as a group leader or lecturer, attempting instead to clarify the group processes using incidents as examples to clarify general points or provide feedback. The group action, overall, is the goal as well as the process. Sensitivity training Program comprises three steps shown in below mentioned figure:

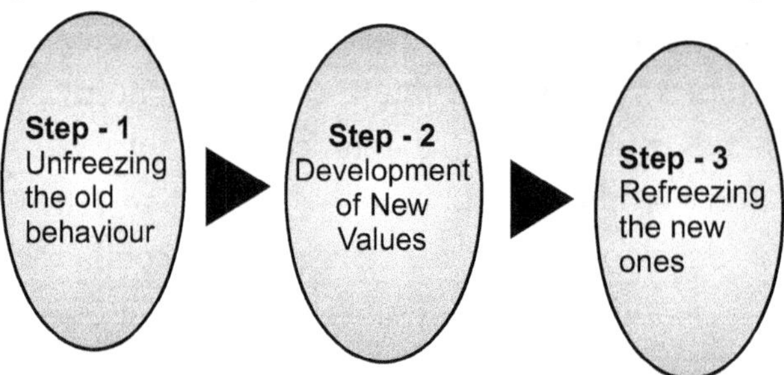

Fig. 3.3: Procedure for Sensitivity Training

- **Transactional Analysis:** It provides trainees with a realistic and useful method for analyzing and understanding the behaviour of others. In every social interaction, there is a motivation provided by one person and a reaction to that motivation given by another person. This motivation reaction relationship between two persons is known as a Transaction.

3.18 Difference between Training and Development

Sr. No.	Training	Development
1.	Training is the learning process for new employees in which they get to know about the key skills required for the job.	Development is the training process for the existing employees for their all round development.
2.	Training is Short Term Process i.e. 3 to 6 months	Development is continuous process and hence it is for long term.
3.	Training focuses on developing skills and knowledge for the current job.	Development focuses on building knowledge, understanding and competencies for overcoming with future challenge.
4.	Training has limited scope, means it is specific job oriented	Development is career oriented and hence its scope is comparatively wider than training.
5.	In Training, Trainees gets trainer who instructs them at the time of training.	In Development, the manager self directs himself for future training.
6.	In Training, many individuals collectively attends the training programmes	Development is self-assessment procedure and hence one person is responsible for one's own development.

3.19 Training and Development Process

Every organization whether profit or non-profit, public or private or government, needs to have well trained and experienced employees to perform the activities in order to achieve the organizational goals. Training is necessary to enhance the skill levels and increase the versatility and adaptability of employees. Inadequate job performance or a decline in productivity or changes resulting of the job redesigning or a technological breakthrough requires some type of training and development efforts.

A training process involves the following steps:-

Adapted from : https://www.businessmanagementideas.com/human-resource-management-2/training-process/training-process/20183

Identifying Training Needs

Establish Specific Objectives

Select Appropriate Methods

Implement Programmes

Evaluate Programme

Feedback

Fig. 3.4: Steps in Training Process

1. **Identifying Training Needs:** Training need is a difference between standard performance and actual performance. Hence, it tries to bridge the gap between standard performance and actual performance. The gap clearly underlines the need for training of employees. Hence, under this phase, the gap is identified in order to assess the training needs.

2. **Establish Specific Objectives:** After the identification of training needs, the most crucial task is to determine the objectives of training. Hence, the primary purpose of training should focus to bridge the gap between standard performance and actual performance. This can be done through setting training objectives. Thus, basic objective of training is to bring proper match between man and the job

3. **Select Appropriate Methods:** Training methods are desired means of attaining training objectives. After the determination of training needs and specification of objectives, an appropriate training method is to be identified and selected to achieve the stated objectives. There are number of training methods available but their suitability is judged as per the need of organizational training needs.

4. **Implement Programmes:** After the selection of an appropriate method, the actual functioning takes place. Under this step, the prepared plans and programmes are implemented to get the desired output. Under it, employees are trained to develop for better performance of organizational activities.

5. **Evaluate Programmes:** It consists of an evaluation of various aspects of training in order to know whether the training program was effective. In other words, it refers to the training utility in terms of effect of training on employees' performance.

6. **Feedback:** Finally, a feedback mechanism is created in order to identify the weak areas in the training programme and improve the same in future. For this purpose, information relating to class room, food, lodging etc., are obtained from participants. The obtained information, then, evaluated, and analyzed in order to mark weak areas of training programmes and for future improvements.

3.20 Training Need Assessment

Training Need Assessment is the essential part of an organization for an employee. Training Need Assessment Process refers to process which determines the gap which exist between what is required from person to perform job proficiently and what they exactly know about the job. It serves as a diagnostic tool for determining what training needs to be developed to help individuals and the organization to accomplish their goals and objectives. This assessment identifies areas where the employees need to improve their knowledge, skills and abilities. Once the training needs are identified, then you need to determine/develop objectives to be accomplished by the training. These objectives will form criteria for measures of success and utility. This analysis can be performed by managers who are able to observe their staff and make recommendations for training based on performance issues or gaps between performance and objectives. This analysis can also be performed on an organization-wide level by Training and Development managers who survey the organization to identify needs. The reasons for conducting training needs assessment are as follows:

- To decide what specific training each employee needs and how will it improve his job performance.
- To determine the content and scope of training.
- Determine the desired training outcomes.
- To provide a basis of measurement.
- To gain support of the management.
- To analyze if training will make a difference in productivity and in the bottom line; and
- To differentiate between the need for training and organizational issues.

Training needs assessment helps to analyze the effectiveness of an organization to achieve optimal performance as well as determine the strength and weakness of the employee. If the training need assessment is done correctly, it will ensure the solution and address the real issues and effectively focus on the appropriate resources, time and effort directed towards finding a solution.

Steps in Training Needs Identification:

The steps in identification of training needs generally include:

1. Performing gap analysis.
2. Prioritizing the needs, and
3. Developing action plan.

1. **Performing Gap Analysis:** The first step in the needs assessment process is to identify the needs. It is used to check the actual performance of organizations and people against existing standards or to set new standards. The gap between the current and the required skill will identify needs, purpose and objectives of the training.

2. **Prioritizing the Needs:** The results of gap analysis are then discussed with the top management to prioritize the needs. Needs of relatively lesser importance receive lower priority.

3. **Developing Action Plan:** After prioritizing the needs, the training manager of the organization prepares the action plan which consists of setting the objectives, identifying the suitable training methodology, identifying the resource persons, estimating the cost for the training programme and finalizing the dates for the training programme.

3.21 Evaluation of Training Effectiveness

Pragmatic Insights: The Major concern of HR managers today is to evolve tools to measure the HR functions including Training. Of course it is essential for managers to evaluate the effectiveness of training to justify the cost and utility of training programme. However the basic question arises is that at the time of training evaluation are: What is to be measured? How it is to be measured? And when it is to be measured? Each company may address the questions in its own way. As Far as Tata Business support is concerned, it adopts Jim Kirkpatrick's framework for the evaluation of training programme. It evaluates training efficiency by analyzing trainee feedback and evaluating performance scores, productivity levels, quality scores and actual knowledge and skills gained at the time of job training.

Evaluation literally means the assessment of value or worth. It would simply mean the act of judging the activity in terms of set criteria for it.

Evaluation leads to control which means deciding whether or not the training was worth the effort and what improvements are required to make it even more effective. Training Evaluation is of vital importance because monitoring the training function and its activities is necessary in order to establish its social and financial benefits and costs. Evaluation of training within work settings can assist a trainer/organization in learning more about the impact of training. It is important to understand the purpose of evaluation before planning it and choosing methods to do it. Some advantages of using evaluations are difficult to directly witness, but when done correctly they can impact organizations in positive ways. Training Evaluation is the process of deep examination and analysis of:

- Selecting measures.
- Gathering information based on those measures.
- Comparing what participants learn to certain goals or expectations.

Evaluation is a process to determine the relevance, effectiveness, and impact of activities in light of their objectives. In evaluating a training and development programme, one needs to consider that most training and development activities exist in a larger context of projects, programmes, and plans.

"Training Evaluation is a systematic process of collecting information for and about training activity which can then be used for guiding decision making and for assessing the relevance and effectiveness of various training components."

According to Hamblin Evaluation of training refers to "Any attempt to obtain information (feedback) on the effects of training programme and to assess the value of training in the light of that information for improving further training."

The Major Objectives of Evaluation of Training are:

- To validate training and development as a business tool.
- To justify the costs incurred in training and development
- To help improve the design of training and development programme.
- To help in selecting training and development methods

The main purpose of Evaluation of Training Are:

At Micro Level	At Macro Level
To measure a specific training and development programme's and its impact on business.	To assess training and development programme's business impact as a whole.
To Look at the benefit of specific elements of the programme, or of the training model for a specific issuer.	To facilitate selection of training and development programme's performance metrics related to organization's goals and objectives.
To Link specific training and development programme's impact on the organization's goals and objectives.	To get at the business impact measure through direct correlation to organization's goals and objectives.

3.22 Model of Training- Kirkpatrick Model

Dr. Donald Kirkpatrick's 1975 book Evaluating Training Programs defined his originally published ideas of 1959, thereby further increasing awareness of them, so that his theory has now become arguably the most widely used and popular model for the evaluation of training and learning. Kirkpatrick's four-level model is now considered an industry standard across the HR and training communities. The four levels of training evaluation model were later redefined and updated in ***Kirkpatrick's 1998 book, Evaluating Training Programs: The Four Levels.***

The Four levels of Kirkpatrick's evaluation model essentially measure: ·

> - **Level 1 - Reaction:** Measures how participants react to the training (e.g., satisfaction?)
> - **Level 2 - Learning:** Analyzes if participants understood the training (e.g., increase in knowledge, skills or experience?).
> - **Level 3 - Behaviour:** Looks as if participants are utilizing what they learned at work (e.g., change in behaviours?)
> - **Level 4 - Results:** Determines if the material had positive impact on the business/ organization.

Adapted from: https://educationaltechnology.net/kirkpatrick-model-four-levels-learning-evaluation/

The model can be implemented before, throughout, and following training to show the value of training to the business. As shown in the above figure the four levels of training form a hierarchy, meaning the lower levels are pre- requisites for higher levels. In other words, if one of the lower level measures is not affected then those measures that follow will not be affected as well.

1. *Reaction* measures whether the employees appreciated the training and facilities. It is usually measured by questionnaires.
2. *Learning* measures whether the employees know more than they did prior to undergoing training. Series of tests helps to identify learning.
3. *Behaviour* measures what employees do on the job after training. Behavioural impact is measured through performance appraisal.
4. *Evaluation of results* looks at the overall outcomes of the training and the impact that the training has on productivity, efficiency, quality, customer service or any other dimensions. This can be measured by sales figures, production, consumer survey or any other means that correspond to the firm's performance measures.

Despite its age, the Kirkpatrick Evaluation Model is still one of the most common training evaluation methods today. The key to using it effectively is to make training evaluation an integral part of your training design from the beginning. By using the Kirkpatrick 4 levels effectively, organizations can develop training initiatives that are effective and impactful and are directly tied to measurable outcomes.

3.23 E- Learning

E-Learning is generally related to the planned use of networked information and communication technology in learning. It is known by several names such as Online learning, Virtual learning, Network Web based learning, and distributed learning. It is also called as "Just In Time Training as it is provided anytime, anywhere in the world where it is needed.

It is commonly referred to intentional use of networked information and communications technology in teaching and learning. It means the using of electronic applications and processes to learn. It applications and processes include Web based learning, Computer Based learning, Virtual Classrooms and Digital Collaborations. E-Learning content is delivered via Internet, Intranet/Extranet, audio or video tape, satellite TV and CD-ROM. A high speed internet connection is an essential prerequisite for widespread E-learning.

E-Learning is one of the successful training programme delivery systems. Since it is Internet learning programme with online instructions, trainees in the E-Learning mode are not constrained by the problems of space and distance. The features of animation and multimedia can make the demonstrations more vibrant and attractive. Virtual reality is distinct feature of E-Learning that allows the trainees to see the objects. Most of the E-Learning is self paced. It is the fastest growing medium of training as the workforce becomes more educated and versatile. E-Learning is convenient as it serves as a supplement for classrooms lectures and demonstrations in training programmes in India.

Pragmatic Insight of E-Learning: A Training Techniques at Aditya Birla Group

Thought the adoption of E-Learning as a training tool is less in India as compared to the International trends, many organizations have just begun to realize the versatility of E-Learning as an important training technique to impart knowledge and skills to their employees. In fact, it enables the trainees to choose the most convenient time and place to learn the relevant skills. The effectiveness of E-Learning can also be increased substantially by making use of graphics, animations and videos. E-Learning, as an online instructions method is a handy tool to train the educated and empowered employees of today. A growing number of companies in India are extensively using Web-based learning kits to help their employees get trained in self paced and individualized fashion.

The well known Aditya Birla Group is a case in point. It has been employing the E-Learning techniques effectively to prepare its employees for better performance and higher assignments. In addition to E-Learning, it has adopted on the job training and structured classroom training to train its employees.

3.23.1 Types of E-Learning

E-Learning is not stand alone term. There are several terms related to E-Learning. Brief descriptions of these terms are given below:

- **Online Learning:** It refers to the learning and other supportive resources that are available through computer.
- **Web- Based Learning:** It is a Training based on the learning resources available on the Intranet, Extranet or Internet
- **Technology Based Learning:** It refers to any forms of training based on technologies like classrooms, televisions, audiotape and print i.e. training other than that given in conventional classroom.
- **Computer Based Learning:** It means presenting courses on a computer. In this case computer is not linked to any network or to learning resources outside the course.

Points to Remember

1. Performance Management is a comprehensive approach that involves the maximum amount of dialogue among all the stakeholders.
2. Performance appraisal on the other hand is primarily a top-down assessment for grading/rating employee's performance periodically.
3. The steps used in performance appraisal are: Setting the Performance Standards, Communicating the Standards, Measuring the Actual Performance, Comparing Actual Performance With Desired Performance, Providing Feedback, Taking Corrective Actions.
4. The performance appraisal methods are Traditional and Modern methods. Further Traditional methods are: Essay Appraisal Method, Grading Method, Ranking Method, Checklist Method, Rating Scales, Critical Incident Method, Force Choice Method, Paired comparison Method, Confidential Report Method.
5. Modern Methods of Performance Appraisal are: Assessment Centre, MBO Method, Human Resource Accounting Method, BARS Method, 360 degree Feedback Method, Computerized and Web based performance appraisal, Psychological Appraisals
6. The purpose of performance appraisal are as follows: Provide Continuous Feedback, Measure Performance accurately, Provides Clarity of expectation and actual results, Identify areas of weakness of employees, Determining Training and Developmental needs, Provide Career Path, Determine promotion of employees, Taking corrective actions, Decide Termination and Retention of employees, Evaluate effectiveness of HRM functions, Decide salary and rewards, Reduces Grievances, Openness in Communication, Motivate performance, Improves decision making ability.

7. The term "Potential" is typically used to suggest that an individual has the qualities (e.g. characteristics, motivation, skills, abilities, experiences etc.) to effectively perform and contribute in broader or different roles in the organization, at some point in the future. Potential is associated with possibilities for the future rather than with problems in current performance.

8. Objectives of Potential Management are as follows: Identification of Employees Having Capabilities to Perform Higher Level Jobs, Assessment of General Potential, Identification of Training Needs of Employees, Implementing Succession Planning Activities, Assisting Employees in Personal Development Process, Helping Organization to decide its Strategy, Helping Organization to Survive, Grow and Develop.

9. Training is learning process that helps employees to acquire new knowledge and the skills required to perform their present jobs efficiently.

10. Development refers to the overall holistic and educational growth and maturity of people in managerial positions.

11. Objectives of Training and Development are: To Enhance Knowledge of Employees, To Improve Job Related Skills, To Develop Proper Job-Related Attitudes, To Prepare for Higher Responsibilities, To Facilitate Organizational Changes.

12. Training methods are categorized into two groups: On the Job methods: It refers to the methods that are applied at the workplace, while the employee is actually working. And Off the Job methods: It refers to the methods that are used away from workplaces

13. On the Job Training includes: Job Rotation, Coaching, Mentoring, Job instruction Technology, Apprenticeship, Understudy while Off the Job Training includes Lectures and Conferences, Vestibule training, Simulation exercises, Sensitivity Training, Transactional Training.

14. The steps which are related with Training and Development process are: Identifying training needs, Establish specific objectives, Select Appropriate Methods, Implement Programmes, Evaluate Programmes, Feedback.

15. Training need assessment is done through three steps which are as follows: Performing gap analysis, Prioritization of needs and Developing action plans.

16. Evaluation leads to control which means deciding whether or not the training was worth the effort and what improvements are required to make it even more effective. Training Evaluation is of vital importance because monitoring the training function and its activities is necessary in order to establish its social and financial benefits and costs.

17. The Four levels of Kirkpatrick's evaluation model essentially measure: Reaction, Learning, Behaviour and Results.

18. E-Learning means use of electronic applications and processes to learn the relevant skills. The elements of E-Learning are Online learning, Web Based Training, Technology based training and Computer based training.

Questions for Discussion

1. What Is Performance Appraisal and Performance Management?
2. Describe in detail the steps involved in the process of Performance Appraisal.
3. Explain in details the methods of Performance Appraisal.
4. What is Potential Management? Explain its objectives.
5. Why an organization feels necessary to measure performance?
6. Difference between Performance Appraisal and Performance Management
7. What is Training and Development? Explain in detail the objectives of it.
8. Evaluate the different steps involved in employee training process.
9. Explain in detail methods of Training.
10. Identify the suitable Training Method for following company:
    - ✓ IT Company.
    - ✓ Pharmaceutical Company.
11. Explain the meaning of Evaluation of training effectiveness.
12. Differentiate between Training and Development.
13. Explain critically the concept of E-Learning as a Training programme.
14. "Training is not an Expense but a long term investment on the people". Discuss.
15. Explain with diagrammatic presentation of Kirkpatrik Model in detail.

Questions from Previous MBA Examinations

1. Define Training. What are the different training methods used in organization.
   (April 2017)

Ans. Refer Articles 3.12 and 3.17 of this chapter.

2. Explain the term Training. How it differs from Development. **(April 2017)**

Ans. Refer Articles 3.12 and 3.18 of this chapter.

3. Define Performance Appraisal. Explain the process of Performance Appraisal in detail. **(April 2017)**

Ans. Refer Articles 3.2 and 3.5 of this chapter.

4. What are different methods of implementing Training Programmes.
   (November 2017)

Ans. Refer Article 3.17 of this chapter.

5. What is Training need Assessment? Explain the process of TNA. **(November 2017)**

Ans. Refer Article 3.20 of this chapter.

6. Define Performance? Why it is important to measure performance. **(November 2017)**

Ans. Refer Articles 3.1 and 3.8 of this chapter.

7. Explain various methods of Performance appraisal. **(November 2017)**

Ans. Refer Article 3.6 of this chapter.

8. What is Performance Appraisal? Explain the importance of performance feedback.
   (April 2018)

Ans. Refer Articles 3.2 and 3.4 of this chapter.

Skills Development Exercise for Students

Objective: The main objective is to let you know how to conduct performance appraisal of your employee in an effective manner through role-playing.

Procedure Note: For this exercise, the class will be divided into small groups with each group having one line manager, one employee working under the line manager, one HR manager, and two observers to monitor the performance appraisal interview. The HR manager will coordinate the evaluation process and the two observers will take care of analysis and feedback aspects of the role playing sessions.

Situation: Mr. Ambarnath is the Branch Manager of the Good Luck Life Insurance Company. He was asked by the HR manager to provide the annual performance appraisal report on one of his team member, Mr Vignesh. All through his career, spanning seven years, Vignesh maintained an unblemished record of his performance as a Development Officer. However this year there were several complaints about his attitude and behaviour especially in dealing with the customers. He was reported to be non-chalant and insensitive when attending to the needs of the customers. A discussion with his immediate supervisor about his performance did not help Vignesh cause. Reports from his peers were also negative and confirmed his deviant behaviour. In this situation, Mr Ambarnath has called Mr Vignesh for an appraisal Interview.

Steps in Exercise:

1. Ambarnath speaks to Vignesh and fixes up convenient date for the Interview and passes the information to HR manager.
2. Ambarnath conducts the performance appraisal interview for Vignesh before the two observers.
3. The performance appraisal report is sent to the HR department and subsequently Ambarnath provides his feedback to the HR Manager in person.
4. The observers give feedback on the interview process. The Role plays ends and the general classroom discussion begins.

Case Study

A process of performance management is developed in companies to better shape how employees execute their job responsibilities and complete their work. Ideally, employees should feel comfortable with this process, believing that the communication occurring between managers and workers facilitates the completion of important workplace goals. Unfortunately, many employees become dissatisfied with how their organizations encourage goal-directed behaviour, which can result in poor job attitudes, decreased motivation, and reduced effort on the job. These negative factors lead some companies to seek alternative ways to design and implement performance management systems so that employees are encouraged to work hard in their jobs. Jewelers Mutual Insurance Company (JMI) is one such company that has actively improved its performance management approach, and the results have been very encouraging. Employees were initially dissatisfied with the feedback and goal-setting approaches that were being utilized to manage job performance, so company leaders decided to involve employees in the redesign efforts to create a more viable programme that would be satisfactory for all the parties involved. An outside consultant started the process by interviewing top leaders in the company, and focus groups were used to solicit feedback from various other members of the organization. By utilizing a more participative and inclusive approach, the company was able to identify the problems with the current performance management system and generate greater support for the proposed changes that would ultimately fix these issues. This case illustrates how important employee participation is in the effective management of human resources, particularly when developing a viable performance management system. Several key changes were made to the performance management system based on the feedback received from managers and employees. In particular, inconsistencies in the administration of the performance management system, problems with the rating techniques and forms, and various challenges linking pay to performance were specifically targeted as part of the redesign effort. Such reflection and self-assessment prompted a number of specific improvements to management of job performance within the company. Evaluations are now based on narratives, various metrics of accountability, and job goals. Further, feedback is provided to employees on a quarterly basis, compensation is more strongly linked to individual effort, and the performance management system functions in concert with the other elements of human resource management. The changes made to the performance management processes at JMI Company demonstrate how human resource professionals can work with other staff members to create a system that excites employees and, ultimately, yields greater job performance.

Questions:
1. Discuss how this case illustrates how greater support for a performance management system can be developed through employee participation.
2. Identify some of the ways that performance management systems can be improved based on the experiences at JMI.

References

1. https://www.chegg.com/homework-help/questions-and-answers/read-case-study-2-building-performance-management-employee-participation-answer-2-question-q24007466
2. http://etd.fcla.edu/CF/CFE0002863/Flaniken_Forrest_W_200912_EdD.pdf
3. https://keydifferences.com/difference-between-performance-appraisal-and-performance-management.html
4. https://educationaltechnology.net/kirkpatrick-model-four-levels-learning-evaluation/

Compensation Management

Contents ...

Learning Objectives:

➤ List the objectives, importance and process of Compensation Management.
➤ Explain the concept of wages.
➤ Explain the difference between Wages and Salary components.
➤ Understand the significance of Incentive programme.
➤ List Financial and Non Financial Incentives.
➤ List the objectives behind Fringe benefits.
➤ Types of separations and how to manage them.
➤ Understand the grievance procedure in Indian Industry.

Pragmatic Insights/Opening Vignette: *Arcelor-Mittal:* Compensation Strategy aims at motivating the employees towards organizational goals attainment, encouraging them to develop their skills and competencies continuously, retaining those who achieve performance standards and forcing the low achievers through pay performance sensitivity to improve their performance.

Arcelor-Mittal views its employees as its most valuable assets and adopts four key steps to achieve the required production efficiency. These steps are aligning the organizational structure with the company's goals, ensuring the right people for the right roles, succession planning and development, and effective incentive programmes. The basic elements of Arcelor-Mittal compensations plans are: the basic salary which is competitive with similar organization and also in the median of the market pay range and the above market bonus as a reward for its employees in the years that have good results. The company also offers an Employee Share Purchase Plan to all its employees in different countries along with bonus rewards. To enhance the effectiveness of the compensation plans, Arcelor-Mittal ensures complete transparent and internal equity in pay fixation by adopting a group methodology in job evaluation. It also related pay with performance to achieve the desired performance and efficiency.

Further the executive compensation plans of Arcelor-Mittal consists of fixed annual salary, short term incentives like performance related bonus and long term incentives like such as stock options. In addition to these rewards its executive are also eligible for perks like company acrs, insurance policies and pension plans.

Now that we have discussed compensation management of one of the largest companies in the world, we shall now discuss the relevance of compensation in general.

Compensation Management - A Conceptual Framework

4.1 Concept of Compensation Management

Compensation is always a vexing issue for the HR managers in the management of human resources. They always strive to develop compensation packages that satisfy the interest of both the organization and the employees. But it is tough and challenging task for any HR manager as there is an inherent conflict of interest between the management and labour over the sharing of the earnings of the organization. For instance the management goal is to limit the cost of production by controlling labour costs whereas the employees aims is to earn more from the profession. However the modern management no longer views compensation as merely a reward for the energy, expertise and the time expended by the employees. In fact it considers compensation as an effective tool to accomplish both the organizational and individual needs in a systematic and satisfactory manner. For many organizations, compensation is a vital instrument to attract and retain the best talents and motivate them to give their best for them.

Compensation management, also known as wage and salary administration, remuneration management, or reward management, deals with planning and applying total compensation package. Compensation is the human resource management function that deals with rewards (financial and non-financial as well) employees receive in exchange for performing a task in the organization.

According to Dale Yoder, "Compensation is paying people for work", *"Compensation is what employees receive in exchange for their contribution to the organization".*   **– Keith Davis**

Edwin B. Flippo defines Compensation as *"The function compensation is defining as adequate and equitable remuneration of personnel for their contributions to the organizational objectives".*

4.2 Objectives of Compensation Management

1. **Obtain Capable Employees:** Compensation should be high enough to attract candidates. Pay levels must respond to the supply and demand of workers in the labour market. Sometime to attract capable candidates working at other organizations, premium wages are needed.

2. **Hold Present Employees:** Inadequate compensation may lead to high employee turnover. High employee turnover is not desirable as it costs high to the organization in many ways. Employees work in organizations for a reward. If pay levels are not competitive, some employees quit the firm. To hold these employees, pay levels must be economical as compared to other employers.

3. **Ensure Equity:** To retain and motivate employees, their compensation must be reasonable. Fairness requires wage and salary management to be directed to achieving equity. Compensation management attempts for internal and external equity. Internal equity requires that pay be related to the relative worth of a job so that similar jobs get similar pay. External equity means paying workers what comparable workers are paid by other firms in the labour market.

4. **Reward Anticipated Behaviour:** Pay should reinforce anticipated behaviours and act as an incentive for those behaviours to occur in the future. Effective compensation plans reward performance, loyalty, experience, responsibility, and other behaviours. Good performance, experience, loyalty, new responsibilities, and other behaviours can be rewarded through an effective compensation plan.

5. **Control Costs:** A balanced compensation management helps the organization acquire and retain workers at reasonable cost. An ineffective compensation management may result in underpaid or overpaid employees.

6. **Comply with Legal Regulations:** A comprehensive compensation management reflects the legal regulations imposed by the government and thus ensures compliance.

7. **Enable Understanding:** The compensation management system should such that it must be easily understood by human resource managers, operating managers and employees.

8. **Encouraging Employees:** Compensation management targets at encouraging employees for higher productivity. Research has proved that monetary rewards cannot motivate employees for better performance. However intrinsic factors such as compliment, promotion, acknowledgement, acceptance, status, etc. help motivate employees. Therefore an effective compensation management takes care of these intrinsic factors and help motivating employees to perform better.

9. **Reliability of Compensation:** Compensation management attempts to achieve reliability in compensating employees. It includes compensation on the basis of the criticality of works and performance on jobs. Thus, higher-level jobs (critical jobs) are accompanied with higher compensation. Further, an employee may earn high compensation than his/ her counterparts because he/ she is higher performer.

10. **To be Sufficient:** Compensation has to be sufficient so that employees can fulfil their needs substantially.

4.3 Importance of Compensation Management

1. It tries to give proper refund to the employees for their contributions to the organization.
2. It discovers a positive control on the efficiency of employees and motivates them to perform better and achieve the specific standards.
3. It creates a base for happiness and satisfaction of the workforce that limits the labour turnover and confers a stable organization.
4. It enhances the job evaluation process, which in return helps in setting-up more realistic and achievable standards.
5. It is designed to abide with the various labour acts and thus does not result in conflicts between the employee union and the management. This creates a peaceful relationship between the employer and the employees.
6. It excites an environment of morale, efficiency and co-operation among the workers and ensures satisfaction to the workers.

In short, we can say that compensation management is required as it encourages the employees to perform better and show their excellence as well as provides growth and development options to the deserving employees.

4.4 Compensation Management Process

The compensation management process has various sequential steps as shown:

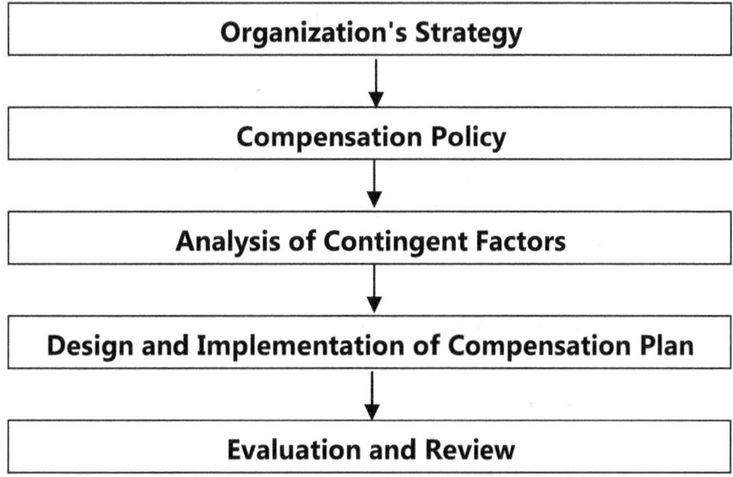

Source: Own

Fig. 4.1: Compensation Management Process

1.   **Organisation's Strategy:** Organisation's overall strategy, though not a step of compensation management is the starting point in the total human resource management process including compensation management. Companies functioning in different types of market/product having varying level of maturity, adopt different strategies and matching compensation strategy and blend of different compensation methods. Thus, it can be seen that organisations follow different strategies in different market situations and align their compensation strategy and contents with these strategies.

2.   **Compensation Policy:** Compensation policy is resultant from organisational strategy and its policy on overall human resource management. In order to make compensation management to work effectively, the organisation should clearly specify its compensation policy, which must include the basis for determining base compensation, incentives and benefits and various types of perquisites to various levels of employees. The policy should be linked with the organisational philosophy on human resources and strategy. Besides, many external factors which impinge on the policy must also be taken care of Job Analysis and Evaluation. Job analysis provides basis for defining job description and job specification. The relative worth of various jobs determines the compensation package attached with each job.

3. Analysis of Contingent Factors: Compensation plan is always framed in the light of numerous aspects, both external and internal, which affect the process of human resource management system. Numerous external aspects are circumstances of human resource market, cost of living, level of economic development, social factors, pressure of trade unions and various labour laws dealing with compensation management. Numerous internal factors are organisation's ability to pay and employees' related factors such as work performance, seniority, skills, etc. Wage and salary surveys may help in analysing these aspects of compensation.

4. Design and Implementation of Compensation Plan: After going through the above steps, the organisation may be able to strategies its compensation plan including base compensation with provision of salary/wage increments over the period of time, various incentive plans, benefits and perquisites. Sometimes, these are determined by external party, for example, pay commissions for Government employees as well as for public sector enterprises. After designing the compensation plan, it is implemented. Implementation of compensation plan needs its announcement to employees and putting this into exercise.

5. Evaluation and Review: Since a compensation plan is affected by numerous factors as described earlier, it is not possible to keep the compensation plan rigid. In fact an effective compensation plan has to be flexible enough to reflect the changes in the internal and external factors which affect compensation plan. Therefore, evaluation and review of implemented compensation plan is very crucial step in the entire process. If it is found through evaluation that current compensation plan is not encouraging employees and not resulting in productive work in the organization then compensation plan must be revisited for necessary improvement as productive output is foremost important objective of the compensation management.

4.5 Current Trends in Compensation

HR professionals should continuously keep an eye on current compensation trends adopted by various organization in their industry. Because such observation may help them to plan an effective and competitive plan in their organization. Here are a few leading compensation trends:

1. **Improving Benefits Decisions:** One of the study found that the majority of respondents (81%) listed managing costs as a top benefits priority, while 50% stated that helping workers to make better benefits decisions was also a top concern.

2. **Breaking up Bonuses:** As part of a way to move towards a more ongoing approach to performance management, some organizations have begun breaking bonuses up into smaller, more regular amounts, according to HR Zone. In doing so, employers can make rewards and praise a more ongoing effort instead of a yearly "event" to support a fulfilling company culture.

3. **Strategically Rewarding Top Performers:** Forward-thinking organizations should aim to offer a variable compensation rate of 7-8% in addition to base pay to top-performing staff members. In doing so, you can use your compensation structure to incentivize high performance and communicate your expectations, which brings us to our next point.

4. **Using Compensation to Communicate:** Organizations are now viewing compensation as a tool that can be used to communicate exactly what's expected of employees. When management is clear on how pay decisions are made, employees can understand the "why" – not just the "what" – behind their pay, which can build trust across the organization.

5. **Seeking Better Technology:** The study referenced by HR Daily Advisor also shows that more than half of employers are looking for better compensation software to reduce workload. If your organization is like the majority, upgrading your compensation tool is one of the best decisions you can make. Not only will it reduce workload; it can also help you stay in line with the other four leading compensation trends listed here. The best way for any company to approach compensation will depend on its organizational strategy, culture, and a number of other differentiating factors. Nonetheless, monitoring compensation trends is essential to making sure the company is paying fairly and competitively in today's job market.

4.6 Factors for Determining Compensation Plan

Defining the "right" compensation can be complicated. Most important factors which are thought to affect compensation rates are described here:

1. **Years of Experience and Education Level:** It is needles to mention that; the more experience and education a candidate has, the higher their expected compensation would be.

2. **Industry:** Industry is also important factor. Because workers working on the same designation and with same profile but from different industry, may demand different wages. This discrepancy may be due to the difference in criticality of their job function in different industries, or it may simply be a matter of one industry being considerably larger than the others.

3. **Location:** Cost of living, a major factor to consider when determining compensation, is largely dependent on location and, more specifically, the cost of housing. This is at least partially why salaries in large urban areas are generally higher than salaries for similar positions in more rural locations.

4. **In-Demand Skill Sets:** When it comes to determining compensation, key skills may be an even more reliable metric to compare against than job title. After all, different

companies may have very different definitions of the same job title. On top of that, many skill sets can apply to a wide variety of roles – all of which are effectively competing for the same talent. That's why it's important for employers to consider the value of key skills when determining compensation.

5.   **Supply and Demand:** It's crucial to be aware of the availability of relevant talent in the geographic region where you're recruiting. If you're recruiting in an area where the demand for a certain skill sets and experience outweighs the supply, you should expect to pay more in order to attract talent.

4.7 Wage / Salary Differentials

A wage differential refers to the difference in wages between people with similar skills within differing localities or industries. It can also refer to the difference in wages between employees who have dis-similar skills within the same industry. It is generally referenced when discussing the given risk of a certain job. For example, if a certain line of work requires someone to work around hazardous chemicals, then that job may be due a higher wage when compared to other jobs in that industry that do not necessitate coming into contact with dangerous chemicals. There are also geographical wage differentials where people with the same job may be paid different amounts based on where exactly they live and the attractiveness of the area.

4.8 Components of Salary

Some of the components of the salary structure include:

1.   **Basic Salary:** Basic salary is the base income of an employee, comprising of 35-50 % of the total salary. It is a fixed amount that is paid prior to any reductions or increases due to bonus, overtime or allowances. Basic salary is determined based on the designation of the employee and the industry in which he or she works in. Most of the other components, like allowances are based on the basic salary. This amount is fully taxable.

2.   **Allowances:** Allowance is an amount payable to employees during the course of their regular job duty. It can be partially or fully taxable, depending on what type it is. Allowances provided and the limits on it will differ from company to company, according to their policies.

3.   **Dearness Allowance:** Dearness allowance is a certain percentage of the basic salary paid to employees, aimed at mitigating the impact of inflation. It is paid by the government to employees of the public sector and pensioners of the same.

4.   **House Rent Allowance:** A house rent allowance is that component of the salary which is paid to employees for meeting the cost of renting a home. It offers tax

benefits to the employees for the sum that they pay towards their accommodation every year. Salaried individuals residing in rented homes can claim this exemption and reduce their tax liability.

5. **Conveyance Allowance:** Conveyance allowance, also known as transport allowance, is a kind of allowance offered by employers to their employees to compensate for their travel expense to and from their residence and workplace. **Note:** In Union Budget 2018, a standard deduction has been introduced in lieu of transport (₹ 19,200) allowances.

6. **Leave Travel Allowance:** Leave travel allowance is eligible for tax exemption. It is offered by employers to their employees to cover the latter's travel expense when he or she is on leave from work. The amount paid as leave travel allowance is exempt from tax under Section 10(5) of Income Tax Act, 1961. Leave travel allowance only covers domestic travel and the mode of travel needs to be air, railway or public transport.

7. **Medical Allowance:** Medical allowance is a fixed allowance paid to the employees of an organization to meet their medical expenditure. **Note:** In Union Budget 2018, a standard deduction has been introduced in lieu of medical (₹ 15,000) allowances.

8. **Books and Periodicals Allowance:** Books and periodicals allowance is a type of allowance provided to employees for helping them meet the expenses associated with purchase of books, periodicals and newspapers. It is tax exempt to the extent of actual expenditure incurred towards purchase of books and periodicals.

9. **Gratuity:** It is a lumpsum benefit paid by employers to those employees who are retiring from the organization. This is only payable to those who have completed 5 or more years with the company. The gratuity amount is paid in gratitude for the services rendered by the individual during the period of employment. According to the Payment of Gratuity Act, 1972, gratuity is calculated as 4.81% of the basic pay. Most firms with a workforce of 10 or more employees come under the Act.

10. **Employee Provident Fund:** Employee Provident Fund is an employee benefit scheme where investments are made by both the employer and the employee each month. It is a savings platform that aids employees to save a portion of their salary each month, from which withdrawals can be made following a month from the date of cessation of service or upon retirement. At least 12% of an employee's basic salary is automatically deducted and goes to the Employee Provident Fund every month. The contributions are maintained by the Employees Provident Fund Organization (EPFO).

11. **Professional Tax:** Professional tax is a tax levied on the income earned by salaried employees and professionals, including chartered accountants, doctors and lawyers,

etc. by the state government. Different states have varying methods of calculating professional tax. The maximum amount that is payable in a year is ₹ 2,500. Employers deduct profession tax at prescribed rates, from the salary paid to employees, and pay it on their behalf to the State Government. The revenue collected is used towards the Employment Guarantee Scheme and the Employment Guarantee Fund.

12. **Perquisites:** Perquisites, also referred to as fringe benefits, are the benefits that some employees enjoy as a result of their official position. These are generally non-cash benefits given in addition to the cash salary. Some examples of perquisites include provision of car for personal use, rent-free accommodation, payment of premium on personal accident policy, etc. The monetary value of perquisites gets added to the salary and tax is paid on them by the employee.

13. **ESIC (Employee State Insurance Company):** If a company has 10 or more employees (20 in case of Maharashtra and Chandigarh) whose gross salary is below ₹ 21,000 per month, then the employer is required to avail ESIC scheme for such employees. The employer's contribution will be 4.75% of gross salary, whereas the employee's contribution will be 1.75% of gross salary.

4.9 Incentives and Benefits

The incentive is a positive motivational influence on a person that helps improve his performance. Thus, it can be said that all the measures taken by the management to improve the performance of its employees are incentives. The incentives can be broadly classified as financial incentives and non-financial incentives.

4.10 Financial Incentives

In today's socio-economic condition money has become a very important part of our lives. We need money to satisfy almost all our needs as it has purchasing power. Thus, financial incentives refer to those incentives which are in direct monetary form i.e. money or can be measured in monetary terms. Financial incentives can be provided on an individual or group basis and satisfy the monetary and future security needs of individuals. The most commonly used financial incentives are:

1. **Pay and Allowances:** Salary is the basic incentive for every employee to work efficiently for an organization. Salary includes basic pay, dearness allowance, house rent allowance, and similar other allowances. Under the salary system, employees are given increments in basic pay every year and also an increase in their allowances from time-to-time. Sometimes these increments are based on the performance of the employee during the year.

2.   **Bonus:** It is a sum of money offered to an employee over and above the salary or wages as a reward for his good performance.

3.   **Productivity linked Wage Incentives:** Many wage incentives are linked with the increase in productivity at individual or group level. *For example, a worker is paid 50 rupees per piece if he produces 50 pieces a day but if he produces more than 50 pieces a day, he is paid 5 rupees extra per piece. Thus, on the 51st piece, he will be paid 55 rupees.*

4.   **Profit-Sharing:** Sometimes the employees are given a share in the profits of the organization. This motivates them to perform efficiently and give their best to increase the profits of the organization.

5.   **Retirement Benefits:** Retirement benefits like gratuity, pension, provident fund, leave encashment, etc. provide financial security to the employees post their retirement. Thus, they work properly when they are in service.

6.   **Stock Options or Co-partnership:** Under the Employees Stock Option Plan (ESOP), the employee is offered the ordinary shares of the company at a price lower than its market price for a specified period of time. These are non-standardized offers and shares are issued as a private contract between the employer and employee. These are generally offered to management as a part of their managerial compensation package.

     Allotment of shares induces a feeling of ownership in the employees and they give their best to the company. Infosys, GoDaddy and The Cheesecake Factory are some of the companies that have implemented the scheme of the stock option.

7.   **Commission:** Some organizations offer a commission in addition to the salary to employees for fulfilling the targets extremely well. This incentive encourages the employees to increase the client base of the organization.

8.   **Perquisites:** Several organizations offer perquisites and fringe benefits such as accommodation, car allowance, medical facilities, education facilities, recreational facilities, etc. in addition to the salary and allowances to its employees. These incentives also motivate the employees to work efficiently.

4.11 Non-financial Incentives

Apart from the monetary and future security needs, an individual also has psychological, social and emotional needs. Satisfying these needs also plays an important role in their motivation. Non-financial incentives focus mainly on the fulfilment of these needs and thus cannot be measured in terms of money. However, there are chances that a particular non-financial incentive may also involve the financial incentive as well. *For example, when a person is promoted his psychological needs are fulfilled as he gets more authority, his status increases but at the same time, he has benefitted monetarily also as he gets a rise in salary.* The most common non-financial incentives are:

1.   **Status:** With reference to an organization, status refers to the position in the hierarchy of the organizational chart. The level of authority, responsibility, recognition, salary, perks, etc. determine the status of an employee in the organization.

A person at the top level management has more authority, responsibility, recognition and salary and vice-versa. Status satisfies the self-esteem and psychological needs of an individual and in turn, motivates him to work hard.

2.   **Organizational Climate:** Organizational climate refers to the environmental characteristics of an organization that are perceived by its employees about the organization and have a major influence on their behavior. Each organization has a different organizational climate that distinguishes it from other organizations.

Some of the factors that influence the organizational climate of an enterprise are organizational structure, individual responsibility, rewards, risk and risk-taking, warmth and support and tolerance and conflict. When the organizational climate is positive employees tend to be more motivated.

3.   **Career Advancement Opportunity:** It is very important for an organization to have an appropriate skill development programme and a sound promotion policy for its employees which works as a booster for them to perform well and get promoted.

Every employee desires growth in an organization and when he gets promotion as an appreciation of his work he is motivated to work better.

4.   **Job Enrichment:** It refers to the designing of jobs in such a way that it involves a higher level of knowledge and skill, a variety of work content, more autonomy and responsibility of employees, meaningful work experience and more opportunities of growth. When the job is interesting, it itself serves as a source of motivation.

5.   **Job Security:** Job security provides future stability and a sense of security among the employees. The employees are not worried about the future and thus work with more enthusiasm. Owing to the unemployment problem in our country, job security works as a great incentive for the employees. However, there is also a negative aspect of this incentive that employees tend to take their job for granted and not work efficiently.

6.   **Employee Recognition Programmes:** Recognition means acknowledgment and appreciation of work done by employees. Recognition in the organization boosts their self-esteem and they feel motivated. For example, declaring the best performer of the week or month, displaying their names on the notice board and giving them rewards, fall under the Employee recognition programme.

7.   **Employee Participation:** Involving the employees in decision making regarding the issues related to them such as canteen committees, work committees, etc. also helps in motivating them and inducing a sense of belongingness in them.

8.   **Employee Empowerment:** Giving more autonomy and powers to subordinates also make them feel that they are important to the organization and in turn they serve the organization better.

4.12 Fringe Benefits

Compensation goes beyond a worker's salary. It includes additional small business employee benefits, known as fringe benefits. Fringe benefits are benefits in addition to an employee's wages, like a company car, health insurance, or life insurance coverage. Any benefit you offer employees in exchange for their services (not including salary) is a fringe benefit.

Common examples of fringe benefits include medical and dental insurance, use of a company car, housing allowance, educational assistance, vacation pay, sick pay, meals and employee discounts. Total compensation includes regular income and all of these paid benefits.

4.13 Employee Separation

Separation of employee occurs when employee leaves the organization for one or the other reasons. Such reason of separation may be voluntary and involuntary. In voluntary separation the employee takes initiative. In case of involuntary separation employee may seek legal protection if he/ she perceives injustice.

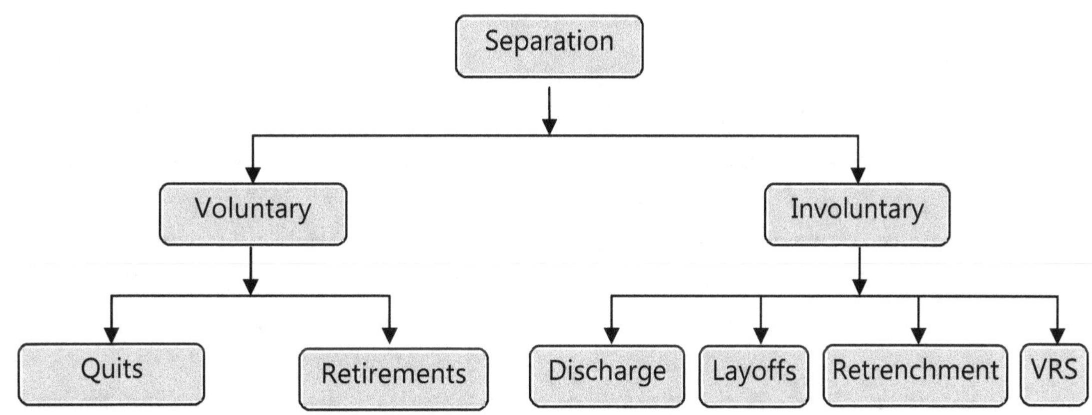

Source: Ashwathappa, K. Text and Cases in Human Resources Management.

Fig. 4.2: Causes for Separation

4.14 Voluntary Separation

Voluntary separation can occur in one of the two forms as below:

1. **Quits:** An employee may take decision to leave the organization due to high level of dis-satisfaction or availability of more attractive job in other organization. Job dis-satisfaction may be due to either intrinsic factor for instance job itself or extrinsic factors such as supervisor, policies at job, advancement opportunities etc. Human resource manager attempts to minimize the number of quits to reduce the employee turnover.

2. **Retirements:** When employee reaches the end of their careers they are said to be retired. The general age of retirement in India varies between 58-60 years. Some employees may be asked to continue the job even after their retirement (only if it is allowed legally) due to lack of skilled employees. Retirement differs from quits as quits can occurs at any point in time in one's career and retirement takes place only at the end of the career. Further, an employee who retires may carry benefits (e.g. bonus) with himself/herself, but if he/she quits the benefits may not be awarded. Moreover, quit is likely to result in hurt feelings with the employer but retirement does not result in such feelings.

4.15 Involuntary Separation

This type of separation may occur due to at least one of the three reasons as below:

1. Organization's inability to maintain employees because of the downfall.
2. Mismatch between job and employee fit due to wrong hiring.
3. Unacceptable behaviour of employee which is affecting the surrounding environment.

Involuntary separation may also be termed as employer sponsored separations.

1. **Discharge or Termination:** When employer thinks that it is no longer desirable to hold an employee any longer, the employer/ organization discharges the employee. Discharge is also termed as termination. Discharge should be the last option that any organization adopts. Because discharge may result in additional costs in recruiting, selecting and training new employee to replace the discharged employee. Furthermore, the discharged employee may badmouth about the organization/ employer.

2. **Lay-offs:** A lay-off is the temporary separation of the employee initiated by the organization. The employee is asked to separate from the current employment for particular period. The period for which the employee will be off the job would be at sole discretion of the organization. Common reasons for lay-offs are:

(a)   Unavailability of power and/or raw materials.

(b)   Accumulation of desired inventory level and low demand in market.

(c)   Non-availability of machinery.

(d)   For any other reason for which organization may not maintain employees for some period.

The employees have to get the compensation for the period for which they are laid off. Organization may lay-off employees by either merit basis or seniority basis. If merit base is used for lay-off then poor performers are laid off first. If seniority is the base then laying off starts with the most junior employee in the organization (or department).

Similarly, for recalling employees, most competent and skilled employees would be recalled if they were laid off on the basis of merit. But in case of seniority basis, the person who laid off lastly would be recalled firstly.

3.   Resignation: A resignation refers to termination of the employment initiated by the employee. An employee may resigns due to any of the many possible reasons. However most common reasons are- securing better employment opportunity elsewhere, (in case of female employee) relocation because of marriage, suffering from ill health etc.

4.   Retrenchment: Retrenchment refers to the separation of employees due at least one of the following common reasons:

(a)   Replacement of labour by machines.

(b)   Lack of demand for products of the organization or one particular department of the organization for long time.

Retrenchment differs from lay-off in that, in the latter, employee is sure to be recalled at the end of the lay-off period whereas in retrenchment the employees leave the organization permanently. Retrenchment is forced on both the employer and the employees thus it differs from discharge as well in that sense.

5.   Voluntary Retirement Scheme or Golden Handshake Scheme: Voluntary retirement scheme is a method used by companies to reduce surplus staff. It is also known as Golden Hand Shake. VRS applies to an employee who has completed 10 years of service or is above 40 years of age. It should apply to all employees (by whatever name called), including workers and executives of a company or of an authority or of a co-operative society, excepting directors of a company or a co-operative society.It has to result in an overall reduction in the existing strength of employees. The vacancy caused by voluntary retirement is not to be filled up. The retiring employee shall not be employed in another company or concern belonging to the same management. The amount receivable on account of voluntary retirement of the employee does not exceed the amount equivalent to three months' salary for each completed year of service, or salary at the time of retirement multiplied by the balance months of service left before the date of retirement on superannuation of the employee. It is the last salary drawn which is to form the basis for computing the amount of payment. Most large public and private sector companies have implemented VRS in recent years.

4.16 Grievance Procedure in Indian Industry

Grievance means any type of dis-satisfaction or discontentment's arising out of factors related to an employee's job which he thinks are unfair. A grievance arises when an employee feels that something has happened or is happening to him which he thinks is unfair, unjust or inequitable. In an organization, a grievance may arise due to several factors such as:

1. Violation of management's responsibility such as poor working conditions.

2. Violation of company's rules and regulations.

3. Violation of labour laws.

4. Violation of natural rules of justice such as unfair treatment in promotion, etc.

Various sources of grievance may be categorized under three heads: (1) management policies, (2) working conditions, and (3) personal factors

1. **Grievance resulting from management policies include:**

- Wage rates.
- Leave policy.
- Overtime.
- Lack of career planning.
- Role conflicts.
- Lack of regard for collective agreement.
- Disparity between skill of worker and job responsibility.

2. **Grievance resulting from working conditions include:**

- Poor safety and bad physical conditions.
- Unavailability of tools and proper machinery.
- Negative approach to discipline.
- Unrealistic targets.

3. **Grievance resulting from inter-personal factors include:**

- Poor relationships with team members.
- Autocratic leadership style of superiors.
- Poor relations with seniors.
- Conflicts with peers and colleagues.

It is necessary to distinguish a complaint from grievance. A complaint is an indication of employee dis-satisfaction that has not been submitted in written. On the other hand, a grievance is a complaint that has been put in writing and made formal.

Grievances are symptoms of conflicts in industry. Therefore, management should be concerned with both complaints and grievances, because both may be important indicators of potential problems within the workforce. Without a grievance procedure, management may be unable to respond to employee concerns since managers are unaware of them. Therefore, a formal grievance procedure is a valuable communication tool for the organization.

Grievance Procedure:

Grievance procedure is a step by step process an employee must follow to get his or her complaint addressed satisfactorily. In this process, the formal (written) complaint moves from one level of authority (of the firm and the union) to the next higher level.

Grievance procedure is a formal communication between an employee and the management designed for the settlement of a grievance. The grievance procedures differ from organization to organization.

1. Open door policy.
2. Step-ladder policy.

1. **Open Door Policy:** Under this policy, the aggrieved employee is free to meet the top executives of the organization and get his grievances redressed. Such a policy works well only in small organizations. However, in bigger organizations, top management executives are usually busy with other concerned matters of the company. Moreover, it is believed that open door policy is suitable for executives; operational employees may feel shy to go to top management.

2. **Step Ladder Policy:** Under this policy, the aggrieved employee has to follow a step by step procedure for getting his grievance redressed. In this procedure, whenever an employee is confronted with a grievance, he presents his problem to his immediate supervisor. If the employee is not satisfied with superior's decision, then he discusses his grievance with the departmental head. The departmental head discusses the problem with joint grievance committees to find a solution. However, if the committee also fails to redress the grievance, then it may be referred to chief executive. If the chief executive also fails to redress the grievance, then such a grievance is referred to voluntary arbitration where the award of arbitrator is binding on both the parties.

How to handle an employee grievance?

1. Establish whether the grievance needs to be resolved formally or informally.

2. Choose an appropriate manager to deal with the grievance.

3. Carry out a full investigation and gather all relevant evidence, sending it to the employee in advance of the meeting.

4. Arrange the grievance meeting, inviting the employee and reminding them of their statutory right to be accompanied.

5. Make sure accurate notes are taken throughout by a person who is not involved in the case.

6. Give the employee the opportunity to explain the details of their grievance and what they would like the outcome to be.

7. Adjourn the meeting consider the evidence before making a decision.

8. Inform the employee in writing of the decision, explaining how and why the decision was reached.

9. Notify the employee of their right to appeal against the outcome of the grievance procedure.

Grievance Procedure in Indian Industry:

The 15th session of Indian Labour Conference held in 1957 emphasized the need of an established grievance procedure for the country which would be acceptable to unions as well as to management. In the 16th session of Indian Labour Conference, a model for grievance procedure was drawn up. This model helps in creation of grievance machinery. According to it, workers' representatives are to be elected for a department or their union is to nominate them. Management has to specify the persons in each department who are to be approached first and the departmental heads who are supposed to be approached in the second step. The Model Grievance Procedure specifies the details of all the steps that are to be followed while redressing grievances. These steps are:

Step 1: In the first step, the grievance is to be submitted to departmental representative, who is a representative of management. He has to give his answer within 48 hours.

Step 2: If the departmental representative fails to provide a solution, the aggrieved employee can take his grievance to head of the department, who has to give his decision within 3 days.

Step 3: If the aggrieved employee is not satisfied with the decision of departmental head, he can take the grievance to Grievance Committee. The Grievance Committee makes its recommendations to the manager within 7 days in the form of a report. The final decision of the management on the report of Grievance Committee must be communicated to the aggrieved employee within three days of the receipt of report. An appeal for revision of final decision can be made by the worker if he is not satisfied with it. The management must communicate its decision to the worker within 7 days.

Step 4: If the grievance still remains unsettled, the case may be referred to voluntary arbitration.

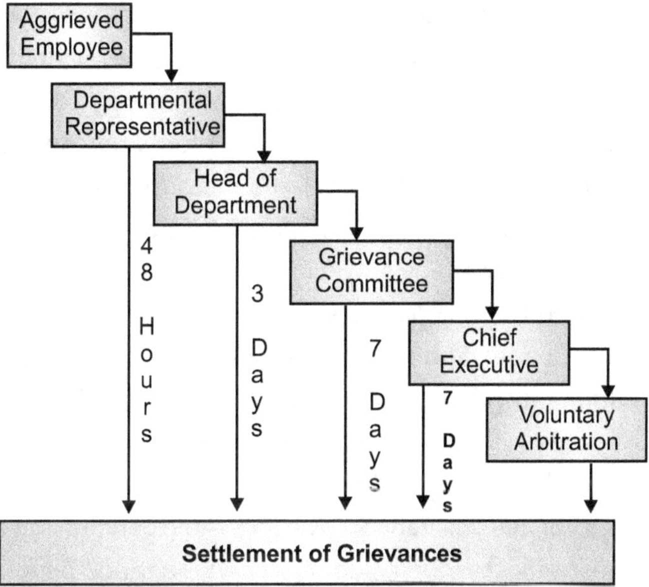

Fig. 4.3: Grievance Procedure in Indian Industry

Points to Remember

1. Compensation is the sum of rewards for the job related efforts of the employees and for their commitment and involvement in the job.
2. The objectives for compensation management are: Obtain capable employees, Hold present employees, Ensure equity, Reward anticipated behaviour, Control costs, Comply with legal regulations, Enable understanding, Encouraging employees, Reliability of Compensation.
3. The compensation can be Direct and Indirect. The elements of Direct Compensation are basic and variable pay, which includes profit sharing, gain sharing and equity plans. Compensation can also be classifies as Monetary and Non Monetary.
4. The Steps include in Compensation Management are: Organisation's Strategy, Compensation Policy, Analysis of Contingent Factors, Design and Implementation of Compensation Plan, Evaluation and Review.

5. Factors for determining Compensation plans are: Years of experience and education level, Industry, Location, In-Demand Skill Sets, Supply and Demand.

6. A wage differential refers to the difference in wages between people with similar skills within differing localities or industries. It can also refer to the difference in wages between employees who have dis-similar skills within the same industry.

7. Components of Salary includes: Basic pay, Allowances ,Dearness Allowances, House Rent Allowances, Conveyance Allowance, Leave Travel Allowances, Medical Allowance, Books and Periodicals Allowance, Gratuity, Provident Funds, Professional Tax, Perquisites, ESIC (Employee State Insurance Company.

8. The incentive is a positive motivational influence on a person that helps improve his performance. Thus, it can be said that all the measures taken by the management to improve the performance of its employees are incentives.

9. Financial Incentives includes Pay and Allowances, Bonuses, Profit sharing, Retirement benefits, Stock Options or Co-partnership, Commissions, Perquisites.

10. Non-Financial Includes Status, Organizational Climate, Career Advancement Opportunity, Job Enrichment, Job Security, Employee Recognition Programmes, Employee Participation, Employee Empowerment etc.

11. Fringe benefits are benefits in addition to an employee's wages, like a company car, health insurance, or life insurance coverage. Any benefit you offer employees in exchange for their services (not including salary) is a fringe benefit.

12. Separation of employee occurs when employee leaves the organization for one or the other reasons. Such reason of separation may be voluntary and involuntary.

13. Grievance means any type of dis-satisfaction or discontentments arising out of factors related to an employee's job which he thinks are unfair. A grievance arises when an employee feels that something has happened or is happening to him which he thinks is unfair, unjust or inequitable.

14. Grievance procedure is a step by step process an employee must follow to get his or her complaint addressed satisfactorily. In this process, the formal (written) complaint moves from one level of authority (of the firm and the union) to the next higher level.

15. Grievance procedure is a formal communication between an employee and the management designed for the settlement of a grievance. The grievance procedures differ from organization to organization such as Open door policy and Step-ladder policy.

Skills Development Exercise for Students

- **Objective:** The main objective is to let you know how to develop wage incentive programme for an organization with the objective of developing ownership interest for the employees.
- **Procedure Note:** For this exercise, the class will be divided into small groups with each group having One HR manager, Two HR Team Members and Two union representatives and two observers of the meetings. The role of Observer is to observe various aspects of the role playing sessions and report on them.
- **Situation:** Ashland is a private sector insurance company engaged in the general insurance business for the past several decades. The company has good business performance record till few years ago. In recent times however the turnover and profitability of the company has dropped considerably due to entry of several new insurance companies in the business. The company begins to offer their insurance products at the cheaper rates as their operating cost was much less. Ashland's labour cost always remained high due to the presence of a large proportion of employee remuneration of fixed nature, for example, the basic salary. The Management was unhappy about the compensation policy which offered more fixed pay and less variable pay like wage incentives schemes. It wanted the HR department to rework its compensation package and make them more performance based. It also instructed the HR people to develop gain and profit sharing plans with the aim of increasing the performance of employees and profitability of business.

Steps in Exercise:

- The HR Manager meets the Union representative to known their views on the proposed changes to the existing compensation policies.
- The HR Manager convenes a meeting attended by the two HR team members to finalise the changes to be incorporated in the compensation policies. The updated compensation policy will subsequently to be sent to the top management for approval.
- The observers will analyse the performance of the members in the role playing session and give them feedback.

Questions for Discussion

1. What do you understand by separations? Explain types of separations.

2. Which separation-voluntary or involuntary- lead to high attrition rates?

3. Describe the effectiveness of VRS in trimming an organization's employee strength.

4. Why VRS evoked mixed response everywhere?

Questions from Previous MBA Examinations

1. What is compensation? State the factors that affect compensation.   **(April 2017)**

Ans. Refer Articles 4.1 and 4.6 of this chapter.

2. Write short notes: **(April 2017)**

   (i)   Difference between termination and resignation

Ans. Refer Article 4.15 of this chapter.

   (ii)   Lay-off

Ans. Refer Articles 4.15 (2) of this chapter.

   (iii)   Golden handshake

Ans. Refer Article 4.15 (5) of this chapter.

3. What are current trends in Compensation?   **(April 2018)**

Ans. Refer Article 4.5 of this chapter.

4. Discuss the employee Grievance Handling process.   **(April 2018)**

Ans. Refer Article 4.16 of this chapter.

Case Study

Salary inequities at Acme Manufacturing

Joe Black was trying to figure out what to do about a problem salary situation he had in his plant. Black recently took over as President of Acme Manufacturing. The founder and former president, Bill George, had been president for 35 years. The company was family owned and located in a small eastern Arkansas town. It had approximately 250 employees and was the largest employer in the community. Black was the member of the family that owned Acme, but he had never worked for the company prior to becoming the president. He had an MBA and a law degree, plus five years of management experience with a large manufacturing organization, where he was senior vice president for human resources before making his move to Acme .A short time after joining Acme, Black started to notice that there was considerable inequity in the pay structure for salaried employees. A discussion with the human resources director led him to believe that salaried employees pay was very much a matter of individual bargaining with the past president. Hourly paid factory employees were not part of this problem because they were unionized and their wages were set by collective bargaining. An examination of the salaried payroll showed that there were 25 employees, ranging in pay from that of the president to that of the receptionist. A closer examination showed that 14 of the salaried employees were female. Three of these were front-line factory supervisors and one was the human resources director. The other 10 were non management.

This examination also showed that the human resources director appeared to be underpaid, and that the three female supervisors were paid somewhat less than any of the male supervisors. However, there were no similar supervisory jobs in which there were both male and female job incumbents. When asked, the HR director said she thought the female supervisors may have been paid at a lower rate mainly because they were women, and perhaps George, the former president, did not think that women needed as much money because they had working husbands. However, she added she personally thought that they were paid less because they supervised less-skilled employees than did the male supervisors. Black was not sure that this was true.

The company from which Black had moved had a good job evaluation system. Although he was thoroughly familiar with and capable in this compensation tool, Black did not have time to make a job evaluation study at Acme. Therefore, he decided to hire a compensation consultant from a nearby university to help him. Together, they decided that all 25 salaried jobs should be in the same job evaluation cluster, that a modified ranking method of job evaluation should be used, and that the job descriptions recently completed by the HR director were current, accurate, and usable in the study.

The job evaluation showed that the HR director and the three female supervisors were being underpaid relative to comparable male salaried employees.

Black was not sure what to do. He knew that if the underpaid female supervisors took the case to the local EEOC office, the company could be found guilty of sex discrimination and then have to pay considerable back wages. He was afraid that if he gave these women an immediate salary increase large enough to bring them up to where they should be, the male supervisors would be upset and the female supervisors might comprehend the total situation and want back pay. The HR director told Black that the female supervisors had never complained about pay differences.

The HR director agreed to take a sizable salary increase with no back pay, so this part of the problem was solved. Black believed he had for choices relative to the female supervisors:

1. To do nothing.

2. To gradually increase the female supervisors salaries.

3. To increase their salaries immediately.

4. To call the three supervisors into his office, discuss the situation with them, and jointly decide what to do.

Questions

1. What would you do if you were Black?

2. How do you think the company got into a situation like this in the first place?

3. Why would you suggest Black pursue the alternative you suggested?

References

1. https://iedunote.com/compensation-management
2. https://resources.careerbuilder.com/recruiting-solutions/how-to-build-employee-compensation-programs
3. http://www.chrmglobal.com/replies/3544/1/case-study-compensation-and-reward-management.html

$\mathscr{Chapter}$ **5**...

Emerging Trends in HRM

Contents ...

A Brief Introduction on Emerging Trends in HRM

HR professionals have faced more challenges in the last few years than ever before. Recession, competition, technology are impacting workforce and a flexibility to change is becoming the mantra of today's HR strategy. Following are some trends that has been observed:

1. Data Analytics have become a Backbone:

As we enter a new economic reality and, in turn, a new reality in the employment market, the ways in which people-related data are utilized will be critical to justifying risk, creating business capability and driving outcomes such as customer satisfaction and sales. Today's HR analytics tools not only permit managers to gain insights on current workforce performance, costs and services, but to also model "what if" scenarios to anticipate changes in business. Today data analytics plays a key role in every aspect of HR from recruitment, onboarding, employee engagement and workforce productivity to off boarding.

2. Swing to Electronic Onboarding:

Onboarding of new hires will no longer be paper-based. Electronic onboarding solutions are now increasingly popular with their easy to handle user interface and workflows. HR onboarding software helps you attain a paperless workflow and filing system. Onboarding process has been simplified by integrating technology with the use of electronic I-9 forms, E-verify and Digital Signatures. Employee onboarding software will lessen manual paperwork and remove redundancy when collecting data from new employees throughout the hiring process.

3. The Impact of Technology:

Technology has encompassed the way we manage workforce. Cloud-based software and mobile apps are accessible for every aspect of HR, including finding job candidates, keeping tabs on field-service crews, running payroll and managing the entire department. The usage of web-based HR systems is on the rise which enables you to cope multiple worksites from a single location. Geographical boundaries are no longer a constraint as technology enables you to reach the farthest locations with ease. Another influence of technology is the influence of social media. Increasingly employers are resorting to this mode of communication for branding, marketing, recruiting as well as background screening. Data privacy and authenticity are just some issues that come along with using social networks.

4. Retention is the Key:

HR workforce and strategies are also going through a sea of change. The emphasis is now more on retaining employees rather than acquiring fresh talent. Accelerated learning programs, focused individual shorter term development and coaching for extraordinary potentials are some of the things that can be introduced in order to retain talent in your organization.

5. Increasing Importance of Work-life Balance:

What with layoffs, cost cutting and there is an increasing pressure on employees to perform and in some cases work overtime in order to make up for the decreased manpower and resources. Stress levels are on an all time high and awareness on importance of work-life balance is necessary to maintain a healthy workforce. Also there is an increasing blur on workplace and home life as reports, mails and official communication is now available on your mobile phones. Connectivity and networking are on an all time high and working on-the-go is seen more as a way of life than it was ten years ago.

6. Increasing Cost of Health Care Benefits:

Health care benefits rank number one among benefits provided by an organization and increasing costs of health insurance and health care benefits is another trend that is here to stay. As employers struggle with rising healthcare costs, U.S. workers are being asked to shoulder the increase in the cost of health benefits on their own. Experts suggest one way to counter this trend is by improving choices of healthcare benefits thereby reducing costs.

7. Managing the Millennial Generation:

The millennial generation are thriving at the workplace. Millennials are typically team-oriented, banding together to date and socialize rather than pairing off. They work well in groups, preferring this to individual endeavors. They're good multi-taskers, having juggled sports, school, and social interests. All Millennials have one thing in common – they are new in their jobs and need mentoring. The challenge of HR professionals would be to find the right mix to get Gen Xers and Millennials to work together.

With the new year fast approaching, there are a multitude of issues that will continue to impact the workplace and require HR professionals and business leaders to stay ahead of the curve. Whether through technology, legislative changes, or the ever-evolving workforce; what has always worked in the past may not be effective (or legal) any longer. Keeping up-to-date of these changes and designing strategies to address them may make the difference between retaining your workforce or losing them to the competition.

When we think of science fiction, images of flying cars, robot butlers and hover boots oftentimes come to mind. It's easy to overlook that there's science fiction for the business world, too. And just like our favorite movies, some fantastical ideas end up making it into everyday routines.

For tech-savvy companies, they represent a chance to evolve their employee engagement in ways that were barely imaginable ten or twenty years ago. This is particularly true in the area of human resources management, which has been transformed by the advent of social media and virtual sharing.

In 2019 and the near future, HR software is moving beyond its base functionality of benefits management, recruitment, time and attendance, professional development, and other standard features. These features are still integral to the technology, but more advanced tools are emerging. Automation is an overarching theme for HR innovation, with many functions becoming completely digitized, eliminating the need for human involvement.

5.1 HRIS: Need, Advantages and Uses of HRIS

(A) Meaning of HRIS:

Human Resource Information System (HRIS) is a software or online solution that is used for data entry, data tracking and the data information requirements of an organization's human resources (HR) management, payroll and bookkeeping operations. A HRIS is usually offered as a database.

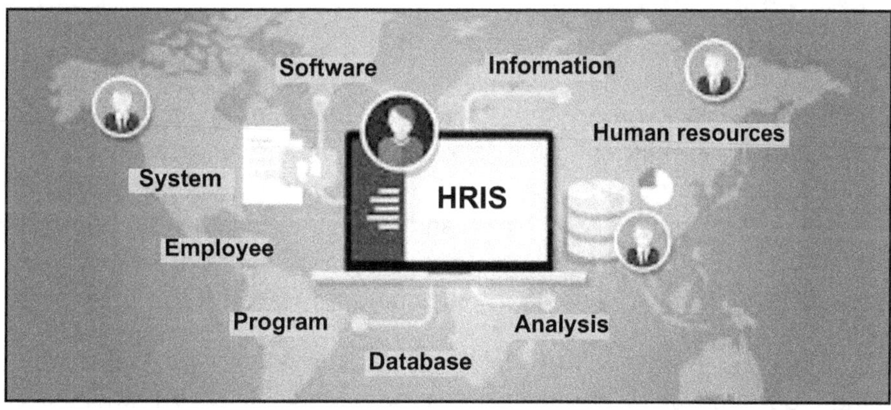

A HRIS, which is also known as a Human Resource Information System or Human Resource Management System (HRMS), is fundamentally an intersection of human resources and information technology through HR software. This allows HR activities and processes to occur electronically.

To put it another way, a HRIS may be viewed as a way, through software, for businesses immense and minor to take care of a number of activities, including those related to human resources, accounting, management, and payroll. A HRIS allows a company to plan its HR costs more effectively, as well as to manage them and control them without needing to allocate too many resources toward them.

In most situations, a HRIS will also lead to increases in efficiency when it comes to making decisions in HR. The decisions made should also increase in quality—and as a result, the productivity of both employees and managers should increase and become more effective.

As an HR professional, you may often feel like you're one person doing the work of many. Well, you're certainly not alone. The Human Resources department of any company, large or small, is charged with a number of critical roles, many of them small but still vital to smooth operations. These responsibilities can include things like formulating the policies of the company, ensuring that the business processes are streamlined, making sure the right paperwork is available and in order in the event of an audit, hiring and firing personnel, and evaluating and motivating the company's employees.

In order to effectively combine the human side of HR with a reliable and efficient organization system, more and more businesses are implementing a Huma Information System (HRIS), computer software that is used to streamline and organize all the HR functions of an organization. An HRIS is able to store all employment records, allowing employers access to metrics on performance management, benefits, compensation and staffing activities.

(B) Need of HRIS in a Company:

(1) Time Management:

With an HRIS, you've got a repository for all your records, documentation and files, and because an HRIS is such an efficient gatekeeper, management becomes much easier as your documents are organized and stored in such a way that they can be easily retrieved. Of course, there is an initial framework to set up and configure, but spending this time up front is worth the effort. Once the HRIS is customized to your specific HR needs, you'll quickly treasure that you have much more time for your work as a human resources professional.

(2) Reports:

One of the biggest advantages of an HRIS is the remarkable presentations and reports it can create for you. Because it stores all of a company's relevant data in one place, a user is able to create an impressive variety of detailed reports that encompass information such as: a current index of job openings, electronic copies of all employees' paperwork, salary and incentive compensation data, annual performance appraisal results and disciplinary actions. For instance, when a manager is ready to hire more staff, he or she can quickly search the HRIS for past job candidates who have a specific set of skills.

(3) Recruitment:

A large number of HRIS systems now have a sophisticated interface that can be used internally by current employees as well as externally by potential job candidates. This type of system makes it possible for resumes to be submitted and other application information to be collected so that it can be easily and quickly accessed by the hiring team. Another benefit of this kind of system is that once resumes have been submitted, a manager can conduct detailed searches to filter information by the candidates' location, educational level, and skill set.

(4) Organization:

An HRIS is particularly valuable when it comes to organization of employee benefits. Businesses are able to streamline the entire employee benefit system, meaning employees and new hires can enroll electronically into benefit plans and log into the system to update and monitor their current coverage. This "self-service" method saves time and money across the board.

It should be clear by now that if you haven't considered implementing a Human Resources Information system, it's time to do so. It's the smart way to save time, keep your records organized, stay on top of employee performance, and bring in the most qualified new hires to your team. While it does take some effort to set up and configure in the beginning, you'll be rewarded in efficient, time-saving effects for years to come.

(C) Benefits of HRIS:

The human resources department within any organization is considered to be highly critical for the entire organization. Its many functions serve as a supportive background for the company by providing everything from skilled and talented labor to management training services, employee enrichment opportunities and more. Since labor is the single largest expense for most organizations, human resources helps companies derive the greatest value from this important asset.

In order to function optimally, however, human resources departments must have the right tools and resources in place. A HRIS can be utilized within the department to help human resources employees and managers improve their productivity and the results of their efforts.

There are many benefits that can be enjoyed after implementing a HRIS into an organization, such as:

1. Expedition of recurring tasks through automation.
2. Improved ability to reach large candidate pools regarding new position openings.
3. Ability to quickly apply higher selection standards to a number of applications.
4. Cutting down on paper work and related materials and storage – often yields cost savings.
5. Ease in distributing up-to-date materials concerning company policies and procedures.
6. Potential for greater employee engagement options.
7. Streamlining of open enrollment for benefits.
8. Empowerment of employees to change benefits info directly as changes occur
9. Improved collaboration throughout organization, even when there are multiple company locations.
10. Improvements in training capabilities through integration with and development tracking features.
11. Scheduling optimisation with an emphasis on compliance and immediate distribution to employees.
12. Decrease of errors within payroll and employee information databases.
13. Improved time and attendance tracking abilities and accuracy.
14. Ability to make more informed decisions in real time by using analytics and integration of organizational data.

(D) Importance of HRIS:

1. Improving HR Productivity

It also influences the overall HR productivity While the HRIS features benefit the organization in many ways, one of the most important of all HRIS benefits relates to the ability of the software program to improve the productivity of human resources employees. These HR systems are highly detailed, and they are designed to enhance and speed up the efforts of HR employees in a number of ways. For example, they can assist with recruitment by simplifying the process of collecting resumes, reviewing candidate information and more.

HRIS systems can also be used to improve productivity related to financial management through payroll processing tasks and benefits administration. These and other related tasks may require numerous hours of manpower each week. However, the time and effort required to complete them can be drastically reduced when some of the tasks are automated through a HRIS system. Tasks that may have required many hours of labour may possibly reach completion very quickly and easily – or sometimes even done automatically – with the software program.

2. Reducing Errors and Maintaining Compliance:

Many HR tasks are highly regulated, and because of this, even a minor error on the part of a human resources employee could result in considerable legal issues and even financial loss for the company. For example, when resumes are not reviewed in a fair and just manner during the hiring process, a lawsuit may ensue. A HRIS can provide guidance to avoid these types of issues before they escalate.

When considering HRIS benefits for your organization, the ability to reduce issues and other related errors associated with human oversight or other factors can be considerable. Furthermore, additional HRIS benefits relate to compliance issues. Some software programs are designed to evaluate compliance with specific rules and regulations—this makes it easier to ensure that your company is in compliance with these laws and regulations. Ultimately, this can improve company reputation and help to avoid penalties.

HRIS analytical tools give HR employees the ability to perform many pertinent calculations with speed. Employees can collect the data needed within a short period of time and then analyze all of the data in a concise and effective manner. Some software programs are designed to create professional reports on metrics and analysis that can help HR professionals to spot issues at a glance.

Companies can immediately enjoy many HRIS benefits once the human resources information system has been implemented. There are several different types of HRIS systems available for purchase, and each may offer different features and functions. Companies should sensibly review the different systems, vendors, and features available in order to find the right program for their needs and budget.

3. Solutions Offered by HRIS Systems:

There are a number of solutions offered to a company that adopts a HRIS. Some of these include solutions in training, payroll, HR, compliance, and recruiting. The majority of quality HRIS systems include flexible designs that feature databases that are integrated with a wide range of features available. Ideally, they will also include the ability to create reports and analyze information quickly and accurately, in order to make the workforce easier to manage.

Through the efficacy advantages conferred by HRIS systems, a HR administrator can obtain many hours of his or her day back in its place of spending these hours dealing with non-strategic, mundane tasks required to run the administrative side of HR.

Similarly, a HRIS allows employees to interchange information with greater ease and without the need for paper through the provision of a single location for announcements, external web links, and company policies. This location is designed to be centralized and accessed easily from anywhere within the company, which also serves to reduce redundancy within the organization.

For example, when employees desires to complete frequently recurring activities such as requests for time off such procedures can be taken care of in an automated fashion without the need for human supervision or intervention. As a result, less paperwork occurs and approvals, may be appropriated more efficiently and in less time.

4. HR and Payroll Factors:

When a company invests in an affordable HRIS, it suddenly becomes capable of handling its workforce by looking at two of the primary components: that of payroll and that of HR. Beyond these software solutions, companies also invest in HRIS modules that help them put the full productivity of their workforce to use, including the varied experiences, talents, and skills of all staff within the enterprise.

5. HRIS Software Popular Modules:

A range of popular modules is available, including those for recruiting, such as resume and applicant management, attendance, email alerts, employee self-service, organizational charts, the administration of benefits, succession planning, rapid report production, and tracking of employee training.

(E) Advantages of Human Resource Information System (HRIS):

A well developed HRIS offers the following advantages:

1. Reduction in the cost of stored data in human resources.

2. Higher speed of retrieval and processing of data.

3. Reduction in duplication of efforts leading to reduction in cost.

4. Availability of accurate and timely data about human resources.

5. Better analysis leading to more effective decision making.

6. Improved quality reports.

7. Better ability to respond to environmental changes.

(F) Uses of HRIS:

The main purpose of maintaining HRIS system is to gather, classify, process, record and disseminates the information required for efficient and effective management of human resources in the organisation.

The various uses of HRIS in an organisation can be listed as follows:

1. Personnel Administration:

It encompasses personal information of an employee. These may include name, address, date of birth, marital status, and the date of joining the organisation. It also contains the name and address of next kin of the employee concern. These information describe the employee.

2. Salary Administration:

One of the functions of HRIS is to provide a report containing information like present salary, benefits, last pay increase and proposed increase in future.

3. Leave/Absence Increase:

HRIS is also used to control leave/absence of employees. This is done by maintaining a leave history of each employee. Every employee can be issued an identity card writing every employee's token number coded on it. Employee's entry and exit from the organisation should be recorded on the identity card. This reduces chances for malpractice or oversight in calculating wages for each employee.

4. Skill Inventory:

Recording employee skills and monitoring a skill data base is yet another use of the HRIS. Such a skill record helps identify employees with the necessary skill for certain positions or jobs in an organisation.

5. Medical History:

The HRIS is also used to maintain occupational health data required for industrial safety purposes, accident monitoring, and so on.

6. Performance Appraisal:

In order to form a comprehensive overview about an employee, HRIS maintains performance appraisal data such as the due date of the appraisal, potential for promotion, scores of each performance criteria and alike. The textual information can be combined with the factual data obtained from the HRIS and the combination of information can be used for imparting training and affecting employee mobility in the form of transfer and promotion.

7. Manpower Planning:

HRIS is used for manpower planning also. It keeps information of organisational requirements in terms of positions. HRIS connects employees to the required positions in the organisation. It is also used to identify vacancies and establish employees thereon. HRIS can also help identify a logical progression path and the steps to be taken for employee progress/ advancement.

8. Recruitment:

Recruitment forms the most essential function of HRM. HRIS helps in the recruitment process in a big way by recording the details of activities involved in employee recruitment. These may include cost and method of recruitment and time taken to fill the positions level wise, for example.

9. Career Planning:

By providing necessary information such as which employees have been earmarked for which positions, HRIS facilitates positional advancement of employees. In other words, HRIS helps in planning for succession.

10. Collective Bargaining:

HRIS through a computer terminal can provide up-to-date relevant and required information, facts and figures and, thus, can facilitate collective bargaining. It can he p collective bargaining as "what if analysis" rather as feelings and fictions. In the same manner, HRIS can also help maintain better human relations in the organization

5.2 HR Accounting: Concepts, Objective, Advantages, Limitations and Method

(A) Concept of Human Resource Accounting:

Human resource accounting is primarily involved in measuring the various aspects related to human asses. Its basic purpose is to facilitate the effective management of human resources by providing information to acquiring, develop, retain, utilize, and evaluate human resources.

Definitions of HRA: Some definition of HRA are as follows:

1. **The American Accounting Association's Committee on Human Resource Accounting:** "The process of identifying and measuring data about human resources and communicating this information to interested parties."
2. **Eric Flamholtz:** "The measurement and reporting of the cost and value of people in organizational resources."
3. **Woodruff:** "Human Resource Accounting is an attempt to identify and report investments made in human resources of an organization that are presently not accounted for in conventional accounting practice. Basically it is an information system that tells the management what changes over time are occurring to the human resource in the business."
4. **Davidson and Well:** "A term used to describe a variety of proposals that seek to report and emphasize the importance of human resources—knowledgeable, trained and loyal employees in a company earning process and total assets."
5. **Stephen Knauf:** "The measurement and quantification of human organizational inputs such as recruiting, training, experience and commitment."

(B) Objectives of HR Accounting:

The more specific objectives of human resource accounting are as follows:

1. To provide cost value date for managerial decisions regarding acquiring, developing, allocating and maintaining human resource so as to attain cost effective organizational objectives.
2. To provide information for effectiveness of human resource utilization.
3. To provide information for determining the status of human asset whether it is conserved properly; it is appreciating or depleting.
4. To assist in the development of effective human resource Management practices by classifying the financial consequences of these practices.
5. To provide cost-value data for managerial decisions regarding acquiring, developing, allocating, and maintaining human resources so as to attain cost-effective organizational objectives.
6. To provide information to monitor the effectiveness of human resource utilization.
7. To provide information for determining the status of human asset whether it is conserved properly; it is appreciating or depleting
8. To assist in the development of effective human resource management practices by classifying the financial consequences of these practices.

Human Resource Accounting is the process of developing financial assessments for people within organisation and society and the monitoring of these assessments through time. It deals with investments in people and with economic results of those investments.

Thus, it essentially involves- (a) measurement and valuation of human resources, and (b) communicating the relevant Information to management and external users.

(C) Objections against the Treatment of People as Assets:

There are several objections to the treatment of people as assets in accounting sense but they have been by and large over-ruled.

They are as follows:

1.   People are not Owned by the Organisation like Other Physical Properties: The first objection is that the people are not owned by the organisation like other physical properties. It is true that people cannot be regarded as slaves or chattels in a modern society. But, it does not imply that the potential benefits of skilled manpower should not be assessed.

There are many organisations where investment in physical non-human capital is negligible, and most of their earnings are derived from the skill and ability of experienced personnel. If the return on investment in any such organisation is calculated on the .basis of only physical, non- human capital, the rate of return would be unbelievably high.

Take for instance, the organisations or consultants, architects and designers, trading firms. The human assets constitute their real and major earning base. The rate of return on investment in these cases, calculated with only gross fixed assets taken as denominator, would show unrealistic scores if the value of human assets is not included.

2.   No Assurance or Future Benefits from Human Resources: Another argument is that there is no assurance or future benefits from human resources. This argument is also not tenable. When fixed assets like plant and machinery are procured, the cost incurred is the estimated potential value of the benefits likely to be derived. Uncertainties of changes in technology and production process and premature obsolescence of machinery are taken into account while assessing their potential benefits and service life. There is no reason why human assets should not be amenable to the same treatment.

3.   Not Recognised by Tax Laws: One more objection to human resource accounting is that it may not be recognised by tax laws. This objection again cannot be sustained. In practice, even now the profit and loss accounts prepared on the basis of existing conventions and concepts have to be redrawn for tax accounting purposes. It should thus be possible to overcome the difficulty of tax laws by incorporating the value of human resources in the financial statements, while accounting for tax purposes may be separately taken care of.

(D) Aims of Human Resource Accounting (HRA):

(1)   Increased managerial awareness of the value of human resources.

(2)   Better decisions about people, based on improved information system.

(3)   Creation of accountability on the part of management for its human resources.

(4)   Developing new measures of effective manpower utilisation.

(5)   Enabling a longer time horizon for planning and budgeting.

(6)   Better human resource planning.

(E) Need of Human Resource Accounting (HRA):

The need for human resource accounting arose primarily as a result of the growing concern for human relations management in industry since the Sixties of this century.

Behavioural scientists concerned with the management of organisations pointed out that the failure of accountants to value human resources was a serious handicap for effective management.

(1) Achieving Long-run Goals of the Organisation: One of the most important aspects of the business manager's job is the use of resources to achieve the immediate and long-run goals of the organisation. This requires resources information of many kinds. The human beings constitute an important asset for an organisation. Without people in an organisation physical and financial resources cannot be operationally effective. But no information about organisation's human resources is available to managers in conventional accounting.

(2) To Reflect the True Level of Business Performance: The measures of the income which are provided in the conventional statements do not accurately reflect the level of business performance. Expenses relating to the human organisation are charged to current revenue instead of being treated as investments to be amortized over the economic service life, with the result that the magnitude of net income is significantly distorted. For that reason conventional balance sheets fail to reflect the value of human assets and hence distort the value of the firm and the rate of return of investment. Distorted measures render assessment of firms and inter-firm comparison difficult.

(3) Conventional treatment of investments on human resources may lead to the erosion of investor's interest through management decisions harmful to the long-run success of an organisation and to the investors' equity.

(4) Traditional accounting involves treatment of human capital and non-human capital differently. While non-human capital is represented by the recorded value of assets, there is no record of human assets corresponding to the human capital of the organisation. But the human assets constitute a vital part of the total capital, in as much as productivity and profitability to business firms largely depend on the contribution of human assets. Two firms may be engaged in the same line of business, use identical physical assets and operate under similar market conditions, but the end results in term of growth and profitability may be quite different due to differences in their human assets. Since the value of human capital is ignored in traditional accounting practice, real assessment of the total value of a firm is not possible.

(5) Expenses incurred by a firm on recruitment, training and development of employees are treated as current costs and written-off against current revenue in the conventional accounts. Expenses on employee welfare and amenities as well as incentive payments for improving efficiency are similarly treated under the present system of accounting.

But, all these expenses are essentially of the nature of investment as the resulting benefits are more often derived over a period of time beyond one year. The conventional treatment of these expenses lead to a general inclination on the part of managers to keep down expenses on human development is welfare. The immediate saving in costs and the resulting profits are achieved neglecting the long-run impact of such a policy on the motivation and morale of the employees.

(6) The impact of management decisions on human assets of the organisation cannot be clearly perceived if the value of human resources is not duly reported in the profit and loss account and balance sheet.

(F) Purposes of Human Resource Accounting:

In the year 1971, renowned management expert Rensis Likert specified the following purposes of HRA:

1. It furnishes cost/value information for making management decisions about acquiring, allocating, developing, and maintaining human resources in order to attain cost-effectiveness;
2. It allows management personnel to monitor effectively the use of human resources;
3. It provides a sound and effective basis of human asset control, that is, whether the asset is appreciated, depleted or conserved;
4. It helps in the development of management principles by classifying the financial consequences of various practices'.

(G) Human Capital – Types (Intellectual Capital, Social Capital, Emotional Capital and Spiritual Capital):

Human resource accounting is in intangible form and is within the inside of human resources. Therefore, there may be different ways in which this can be classified. There are four types of human capital- intellectual capital, social capital, emotional capital, and spiritual capital. Let us briefly discuss these to identify how these contribute to individual effectiveness.

1. Intellectual Capital:

The first element of the human capital is intellectual capital which can be defined at individual level as well as at organizational level. At the level of individual, it refers to his knowledge, skills, and expertise. It may be in the form of specialized knowledge, tacit knowledge and skills, cognitive complexity, and learning capacity.

At the organizational level, intellectual capital consists of both the stock of knowledge, skills, and expertise that members of the organization collectively possess, and the knowledge and expertise that may be embedded in or owned by the organization including patents, information technology based knowledge systems, or specialized processes of work.

Ghoshal observes that "in the recent past, much management attention has been paid to this issue of intellectual capital, and rightly so. Knowledge rather than money is increasingly becoming the key competitive differentiator — certainly in service industries like consulting, investment banking, IT services, and so on, but also in manufacturing-based businesses like pharmaceuticals, consumer electronics, and electrical machinery."

2. Social Capital:

Social capital is the second element of human capital. It is derived from the network of relationships, both internally and externally. From organization's point of view, social capital relates to the structure, quality, and flexibility of the human networks which can be created through cohorts, joint training in which people get to know each other, job rotation through different departments and functions, long-term employment, and internal culture.

The other aspect of social capital is external — built on the relationships with external forces like customers, suppliers, government agencies, etc. However, building external relationships and working on these does not involve taking undue advantages for furthering the interest of the organization. It is used in the context of trustworthiness.

3. Emotional Capital:

Emotionality is one of the five big personality dimensions that affect job performance. In order to develop high level of emotional maturity in people for better performance, psychologists started work on it.

One of them, Daniel Goleman, coined and popularized the term emotional intelligence which refers to "emotional awareness and emotional management skills which provide the ability to balance emotion and reason so as to maximize long-term happiness."

Emotional capital constitutes this emotional intelligence. Thus, emotional capital is the value of emotional awareness and emotional management skills of employees of an organization. Like intelligence quotient (IQ), emotional intelligence is also expressed in terms of emotional quotient (EQ). EQ emerges from mind's status of a person and not from his brain. Thus, it is a psychological phenomenon.

Therefore, IQ and EQ are different phenomena. However, both are not mutually exclusive. A person may be high on both IQ and EQ or low on both. Persons with high EQ are high on self-awareness, self-control, autonomy, confidence, focus, purposefulness, integrity, and motivation.

In today's context, emotional intelligence is being perceived as the most important element in a person's success. For example, while comparing IQ and EQ, Goleman suggests that while 20 per cent success is contributed by IQ, the remaining 80 per cent success is determined by EQ. It is now widely believed that emotional intelligence rather than IQ may be the true measure of human intelligence.

Emotional intelligence plays role in the following areas:

(i)   For filling organizational positions with different types of jobs requiring different levels of EQ.

(ii) Improving quality of work life by adopting rationality in unusual situations like organizational change, stress, criticisms, or similar such events.

(iii) Developing credibility of persons as they make consistent decisions by using their rationality.

(iv) Effective communication through use of appropriate emotions.

(v)   Conflict resolution by not involving emotionally in any conflict.

(vi) Increased leadership effectiveness because of ability to regulate emotions, emotional facilitation of thinking, and ability to express emotions appropriately.

4. Spiritual Capital:

Spiritual capital has been recognized as the latest ingredient of human capital. It has emerged out of workplace spirituality. Therefore, first, let us discuss this concept. Spirituality, in general, is defined in religious term and is related to submission to God. However, workplace spirituality cannot be defined in such an abstract form but is defined in terms of recognition that people have inner life that nourishes and is nourished by meaningful work that leads to realize ultimate goal of life.

Organizations that practise spirituality are concerned with helping people to develop and reach their full potential. Many scholars have derived the meaning of spiritual capital from this theme and have defined it 'what makes life meaningful'.

Operationally, spiritual capital is defined as individual dispositions that manifest as belief in something larger than self, a sense of interconnectedness, ethical and moral conscience, a drive to serve, and the ability to transfer these conceptualizations into behaviors and, ultimately, added value.

Spiritual capital in an organization has the following advantages:

(i)   It frees up higher order potential in individual.

(ii)   It encourages and enhances visioning.

(iii)   It recovers idealism and accountability.

(iv)   It encourages learning and new work models.

(v)   It encourages participation and flattens hierarchy.

(vi)   It paves the way for organizational transformation.

(vii)   It achieves higher personal standards of excellence at ethics with less need for policing.

An HR practitioner has observed about the importance of EQ as such, "whereas with a high IQ, you may get hired, with a high EQ, you may get promoted. But this is a short-term perspective and long-term growth is linked to SQ."

All these forms of human capital are not isolated rather these are interrelated. Therefore, while measuring human capital, all these must be taken together. Human resource accounting makes attempt to measure this capital.

(H)   Human Resource Accounting (HRA) – Approaches or Methods (Cost Approach, Economic Value Approach and Non-Monetary Methods):

There are different angles to HRA, regarding components of costs, investment and value related to employees of an organization. There are two approaches to assign monetary values to these aspects, the cost approach and the economic value approach. The cost approach involves the expenditures incurred by a company regarding an employees like costs of recruitment, selection, placement, training and development, etc.

On the other hand, the economic value approach regards employees as assets and measures the economic value added by the employees to the organization's total worth. It aims to measure the benefits created by HR.

1.   The Cost Approach:

I.   The Historical Cost Method:

According to this method, all the costs incurred in recruitment, selection, placement, training and development of employees are taken into account while evaluating the value of human resources. Some of these costs are direct costs like salaries while costs in terms of time spent in training and development are indirect costs.

This method is simple and easy to understand, though it suffers from many demerits; the biggest one being that since training and development costs are taken into account while valuing employees, highly skilled employees requiring lesser training will be valued lower than those requiring more training.

II. The Opportunity Cost Method:

This method calculates what would have been the returns if the money spent on HR was spent on something else. It was Hekimian and Jones who had advocated this method, also known as the Market Value Method.

This is not a very objective method and therefore is only used for internal reporting. One serious limitation of this method is that it totally disregards the fact that well-trained employees can be easily hired from outside sources, and it would be difficult to measure the opportunity costs related to them.

III. The Replacement Cost Method:

Replacement cost refers to the costs that would have to be incurred if the existing employees were to be replaced by identical ones. When an employee leaves the organization, costs of recruiting, selecting, placing and training the new employee would have to be incurred in order to replace him.

The replacement costs can be viewed from two angles: personal replacement costs and positional replacement costs. Personal replacement cost is the cost that would have to be incurred to replace an employee with a substitute who can provide the same set of services that the employee being replaced might have rendered at various positions he would have occupied during his tenure.

Positional replacement costs are the costs incurred to replace the set of services rendered by an employee in a particular position. This takes into account the position the employee is currently holding as well as the future positions expected to be held by him. The major weakness of this method is that it is highly subjective.

2. The Economic Value Approach:

I. Flamholtz's Model of Determinants of Individual Value to Formal Organizations:

According to Flamholtz, the value of an individual to an organization is determined by the services he is expected to render. The current value of an employee is the present worth of the services that he is likely to render to the organization in future.

As an employee moves from one position to another within the organization, the set of services provided by him changes. While calculating the current value of the individual, the present cumulative value of all the possible services that may be rendered by him during his tenure with the organization is taken.

There are two dimensions to this value:

(i) Expected conditional value- This is the worth that could be possibly realized from the services of an individual over the period of his productive work life in the organization.

(ii)   Expected realizable value- The expected realizable value depends upon the expected conditional value of an employee and the probability that the individual will remain in the organization for the duration of his productive work life. Since the employees may leave the organization any time they wish, it is important to ascertain the chances of their turnover.

II. Flamholtz's Stochastic Rewards Valuation Model:

This model considers the movement of employees in an organization through various roles. This process of progressing through organizational states is called a stochastic process. The stochastic rewards valuation model measures a person's expected conditional value and expected realizable value.

In any organization, employees generate value as they move along organizational roles and render a set of services in different capacities. It is presumed that any employee would move from one state to another over a duration of time; in this model the separation of an employee from his workplace is also considered a state. This is a very sophisticated and complex model that requires extensive information for determining the value of individuals.

III. The Lev and Schwartz Model:

According to this model, the value of human resources is calculated as the present value of estimated future earnings discounted by the rate of return on investment (cost of capital).

The mathematical formula for calculation of value of human resources is as follows:

$$V_y \;=\; \frac{I\,(t)}{(1 + r)^{t-y}}$$

Where,

V = the value of an individual 'y' years old.

I(t) = the individual's annual earnings up to retirement.

t = retirement age.

r = a discount rate specific to the cost of capital to the company.

This is the most commonly used method for HRA used by most companies in India.

IV. Hekimian and Jones Competitive Bidding Model:

In this method, the managers bid against each other for the human resources already available in an organization. The highest bid is taken as the value of the employee. This is a highly subjective method as there are no set criteria to evaluate the employees. The value of an employee is based solely on the judgement of the managers.

3. Non-Monetary Methods:

The value of human resources can be measured by non-monetary methods as well. These methods may be used to supplement monetary methods.

    I.   **Skills Inventory:** This is a simple listing of the education, knowledge, experience, skills of the organization's human resources.

    II.   **Performance Evaluation Methods:** This includes methods like simple ranking method, paired comparison, check lists, graphic rating scales, etc.

III. Potential Assessment: It refers to the identification of hidden skills, talents and abilities in a person which even he may be unaware of. It determines an employee's capacity for promotion and advancement.

IV. Attitude Measurements: These measurements assess employees' attitudes towards their jobs, remuneration, work environment, etc. in order to determine their levels of satisfaction or dissatisfaction.

CASE STUDY HRA at Infosys:

Infosys has estimated the value of its human resources of 91,187 employees, including both delivery and support staff at Rs.98,821 crore for fiscal 2008. This represented a growth a 72 per cent growth over the previous year's Rs.57,452 crore, when the company had a headcount of 72,241 employees. The IT major has used the Lev and Schwartz model to compute the value of its human resources.

The evaluation is based on the present value of the future earnings of the employees and on the assumptions that employee compensation includes all direct and indirect benefits earned both in India and abroad. It also considered the incremental earnings based on group/age and discounted the future earnings at 13.32 per cent (14.97 per cent in the previous year), the cost of capital for computing the HR value.

Education Index:

The company reported a substantial jump in the education index of its employees for fiscal 2008 at 2,51,970 up from 2,03,270 in the previous year, reflecting the rising quality of its employees. The average age of the Infosys employees stood at 26 years in FY07, the same as in the previous years.

(I) Human Resource Accounting (HRA) – Arguments in Favour and Against:

The issue of Human Resource Accounting has always been debated hard and there have been arguments both in favour and against regarding its practical utility and effectiveness.

Argument in Favour of Human Resource Accounting:

The various arguments favouring human resource accounting are as follows:

1. HRA helps to justify human resource as assets in an era of knowledge-based economy.

2. Attaches numerical monetary-equivalent to the true-value of human assets in an organization.

3. Facilitates HR decision-making. HRA provides the HR professionals and management with information for managing the human resources efficiently and effectively. Such information is essential for performing the critical HR functions of acquiring, developing, allocating, conserving, utilizing, evaluating and rewarding in a proper way.

    These functions are the key transformational processes that convert human resources from 'raw' inputs (in the form of individuals, groups and the total human organization) to outputs in the form of goods and services.

4. It also helps the management to understand the long-term cost implications to such decisions. HRA indicates whether these processes are adding value or enhancing unnecessary costs.

5. HRA helps institutional investors in making a more informed financial decision.

6. Finally, in an era where performance is closely linked to rewards and, therefore, the performance of all groups/departments/functions needs to be quantified to the extent possible, HRA helps in measuring the performance of the HR function as such.

Arguments against Human Resource Accounting:

As far as the statutory requirements go, the Companies Act, 1956 does not demand furnishing of HRA related information in the financial statements of the companies. The Institute of Chartered Accountants of India too, has not been able to bring any definitive standard or measurement in the reporting of human resources costs.

(J) Human Resource Accounting (HRA) – Benefits and Advantages:

Benefits of HRA:

1. The adoption of the system of HRA discloses the value of human resources. This helps in proper interpretation of Return on Capital Employed. Such information would give a long-term perspective of the business performance which would be more reliable than the Return on Capital Employed under the conventional system of accounting.

2. The maintenance of detailed record relating to internal human resources (i.e., employees) improves managerial decision-making specially institutions like direct recruitment versus promotions; transfer versus retention; retrenchment or reliving versus retention; utility of cost reduction programme in view of its possible impact on human relations and impact of budgetary control on human relations and organisational behaviour. Thus, the use of HRA will definitely improve the quality of management.

3. The adoption of the system of HRA serves social purpose by identification of human resources as a valuable asset which will help prevention of misuse and under use due to thoughtless or rather reckless transfers, demotions, layoffs and day-to-day maltreatment by supervisors and other superiors in the administrative hierarchy; efficient allocation of resources in the economy; efficiency in the use of human resources; and proper understanding of the evil effects of avoidable labour unrest/disputes on the quality of internal human resources.

4. The system of HRA would no doubt, pave the way for increasing productivity of the human resources, because, the fact that a monetary value is attached to human resources and that human talents, devotion and skill are considered as valuable assets and allotted a place in the financial statements of the organisation, would boost the morale, loyalty and initiative of the employees, creating in their mind a sense of belonging towards the organisation and would act as a great incentive, giving rise to increased productivity.

Advantages of HRA:
1. It helps in giving valuable information to the management for effective planning and managing human resources.
2. It helps in measurement of standard cost of recruiting, selecting, and developing people and organization can select a person with highest expected realizable value.
3. Human resource accounting can change the attitude of managers completely, thereby, they would try to maximize the expected value of human resources and effective use of human resources in the organization.
4. It also provides necessary data to devise suitable promotion policy, congenial work environment, and job satisfaction to the people.

(K) Limitations of Human Resource Accounting (HRA):

There are certain operational problems in human resource accounting because it attempts to measure intangibles. Therefore, subjective factors may play crucial role.

Thus, the major operational problems (limitations) involved in human resource accounting are of the following types:

1. **No well-set Standard Accounting Practice for Measuring the value of Human Resources:** There is no well-set standard accounting practice for measuring the value of human resources. In the case of financial accounting, there are certain specified standards which every organization follows. However, in the case of human resource accounting, there are no such standards.

   Therefore, various organizations that undertake valuation of human capital use their own models. As a result, value of human capital of two organizations may not be comparable.

2. **Unrealistic Assumption:** Valuation of human capital is based on the assumption that the employees may remain with the organization for certain specified period. However, this assumption may not hold true in today's context because of increased human resource mobility.

3. **Dehumanization in the Organisation:** There is a possibility that human resource accounting may lead to the dehumanization in the organization if the valuation is not done correctly or results of the valuation are not utilized properly.

4. **Opposition by Trade Unions:** There is also a possibility that trade unions may oppose the use of human resource accounting. They may want parity of wages/salaries and value of employees. However, many of these problems are of operational nature or of attitudinal nature. These may be overcome by developing suitable organizational climate and culture.

(L) Human Resources Accounting (HRA) – Issues and Concerns:

Human resources accounting (HRA) is an information system that tells the management what changes have been occurring in the HR department of the business over a period of time. HRA also involves accounting for investment in people, their replacement costs, and the economic value of people in an organization.

Organizations can assess how much they can earn from an individual as the intellectual assets of a company are often worth three or four times the tangible asset value. Human capital provides valuable expert services, such as consulting, financial planning, and assurance services, which are in great demand.

In India, very few companies, for example, BHEL, Infosys, and Reliance Industries, have implemented HRA. Infosys, which started showing human resource as an asset in its balance sheet, has been reaping high market valuations. NIIT has been following a similar method called economic value addition (EVA), which helps assess the real value of an employee in the company.

Indian organizations have invested substantially in defining and implementing various processes and systems with a view to handling three main aspects, that is, competencies, commitment, and culture.

Competencies are not restricted to individuals, but are spread over teams, departments, divisions, and small business units (SBUs). They provide the lead and competitive edge to the organization.

The commitment of the employee is a complex factor dependent upon a host of factors, such as reward and recognition, developmental and learning opportunities, mentoring and fault-tolerance levels, etc. in the organization.

Culture is represented by the values and norms articulated and practised by the organization. It improves motivational levels and the commitment of the employees, and helps in instilling a sense of pride amongst the employees. The various instruments used for culture building in the organization include climate survey, value clarification exercises, and vision/mission workshops.

Organizations that inculcate good HR practices reap several benefits. These practices drive organizational growth.

(M) Human Resource Accounting (HRA) in India:

Under the constraints under which the financial statements are prepared under the Companies Act in India, there is no scope for showing any significant information about human resources in financial statements except the remuneration paid to them and the number of employees getting ₹ 36,000 per annum or ₹ 3,000 per month. But there is nothing to prohibit the companies to attach information about the worth of human resources and the results of their performance during the accounting period in notes or schedules.

In India, the concept of HRA is yet to gain momentum. Bharat Heavy Electricals is a pioneer in this direction. A few more organisations like Minerals and Metals Trading Corporation of India, Southern Petrochemical Industries Corporation. Oil and Natural Gas Commission and Neyvell Lignite Corporation are adopting this concept. But the concept is adopted as additional information. The concept of HRA is yet to gain momentum in India. However, beginning has been made.

The following companies do give information of their human assets by following a particular model of valuation of human resources.

These are as follows:

1. Bharat Heavy Electricals Ltd. (BHEL).
2. Steel Authority of India Ltd. (SAIL)
3. Oil India Ltd.
4. Mineral & Metal Trading Corporation of India
5. ONGC
6. Cement Corporation of India
7. Tata Motors Ltd.
8. Associated Cement Company (ACC).
9. Southern Petro Chemicals Industries Corporation
10. Infosys Technologies Ltd.

Human Resource Accounting is a process which involved pinpointing and recording investments put into the human resources of a company but not present in normal accounting practice. It is the process of finding and dissecting data on the workforce and disseminating this data to interested parties.

In simpler terms, it is the term coined to quantify the value and cost of workers to the company they work for. This system involves valuing the worth of workers then recording and systematically presenting the data in the accounts books of a company.

5.3 HR Audit: Concept, Objective, Scope and Process

(A) Introduction to HR Audit Concept:

A Human Resources Audit (or HR Audit) is a comprehensive method (or means) to review current human resources policies, procedures, documentation and systems to identify needs for improvement and enhancement of the HR function as well as to assess compliance with ever-changing rules and regulations.

The HR Audit is the process of evaluating the performance of Human Resource Department and its activities undertaken, and the policies followed towards the accomplishment of organizational goals.

The HR Audit is conducted to identify the lapses, shortcomings, gaps in the implementation of HR functions and suggesting the remedial actions, if any.

HR audit can be partial or comprehensive. In the former type of Audit, few areas of HR are monitored, whereas in the latter a complete Human Resource check-up is carried out such as admin, employee details, handbook, performance management, training programmes, termination procedures, etc.

(B) Approaches to HR Audit:

Following are the approaches that can be adopted by an auditor to evaluate the performance of the HR department:

1. **Comparative:** In this approach, the auditor identifies any company usually the competitor's company as a model. Then the results of the organization are compared with that of the model company.

2. **Outside Authority:** The auditor uses the standard set as a benchmark by the outside consultant and then compares the organization's performance with that.

3. **Statistical:** Under this approach, the auditor develops the statistical measures of performance for the existing organization's information, such as turnover rates, absenteeism.

4. **Compliance:** Here the auditor checks the past actions of the company to ensure that those activities comply with the legal requirements and is in line with the company's policy and procedures.

5. **Management by Objective:** Under this approach, the auditors check the performance of HR personnel against the goals set by the top management.

   It is recommended to have an HR audit once in a year so that, the performance of the HR department in terms of its recruitment and selection process, compensation plan, grading system, layoff schemes and other HR functions can be checked. By doing so, it can be ensured that Human resource practices are carried out at its best and is reducing the organization's liability as a whole.

(C) Human Resource Audit – Meaning:

The term audit is normally associated with financial accounting and refers to the official examination and verification of a company's financial and accounting records. HR audit is a similar concept in the field of Human Resource Management.

HR audit involves examining and reviewing the organization's existing policies, procedures and practices regarding recruitment and selection, orientation and placement, training and development, job analysis and design, job evaluation, compensation, morale and motivation, employee health and safety, social welfare, industrial relations, etc.

According to Eric Flamholtz, "Human Resource Audit is a systematic assessment of the strengths, limitations, and developmental needs of its existing human resources in the context of organizational performance."

Normally, in an organization, not all HR policies are formal and written; there are many informal policies, not officially documented. The HR audit involves the review of all the HR policies, procedures and practices currently adopted by the organization, irrespective of whether they are formal or informal.

The audit also helps to check that the company complies with the legal requirements and regulations regarding employees as laid down by the government of the country. By means of an audit, the company can determine its strengths and weaknesses in the area of HRM and plan accordingly to improve its processes and procedures related to the human resource function.

Human Resource Audit also called Personnel Management Audit is well practised in Western developed countries. In India, there is no lull audit like financial audit of the personnel or Human Resource activities in an organisation. Audit is evaluation, examination, review and verification of completed activities, to see whether they represent a true state of affairs of the activities in the department audited.

Human Resource audit refers to an examination and evaluation of policies, practices, procedures to determine the effectiveness and efficiency of the Human resource management and to verify whether the mission, objectives, policies, procedures, programmes have been followed, and expected results achieved. The audit also makes suggestions for future improvement as a result of the measurement of past activities.

It helps essentially in evaluating the various HR practices and processes in an organization against the set standards. An HR audit involves devoting time and resources to taking an intensely objective look at the company's HR policies, practices, procedures and strategies to protect the company, establish best practices and identify opportunities for improvement.

A Human Resources Audit is a comprehensive method (or means) to review current human resources policies, procedures, documentation and systems to identify needs for improvement and enhancement of the HR function as well as to ensure compliance with ever-changing rules and regulations.

The HR audit shall include evaluating:

1.	Job Analysis,	2.	Recruitment,
3.	Selection,	4.	Performance Management,
5.	Performance Appraisals,	6.	Performance Feedbacks,
7.	Competency Mapping,	8.	Training Process,
9.	Compensation,	10.	Rewards Management,
11.	Benefits Management,	12.	Employee Relations,
13.	Workplace Safety,	14.	Best Practices,
15.	Managerial performance,	16.	Supervisory Performance,
17.	Leadership at various levels,	18.	HR Business Partner Role,
19.	HR Strategic Initiatives,	20.	Legal HR issues.

Definitions of HR Audit:

> 1. *"HR audit evaluates the HR activities in an organization with a view to their effectiveness and efficiency."* — **Biles and Schuler**
> 2. *"HR audit is concerned with the gathering, analysing information, and then deciding what actions need to be taken to improve performance."* — **Storey and Sission**
> 3. *"HR audit is a tool to measure an employer's compliance with its legal obligations in managing its workforce and chart any corrective actions that might be needed."* — **Stephen F.Ruffino**
> 4. *"HR audit is an examination of the human resources policies, practices, and systems of a firm (or division) to eliminate deficiencies and improve ways to achieve goals."* — **Schwind, Das and Wagar**

(D) Objectives of Human Resource Audit:

HR audit is a comprehensive analysis of HR functions, systems, policies and procedures of an organization.

The major objectives of HR audit are as follows:

1. To conduct an independent, objective, systematic and critical examination of HR functions of an organization.
2. To assess the general environment and performance efficiency in HR department.
3. To check for any deviations from standards and devise appropriate strategies and corrective actions in HR related areas.
4. To check for alignment of HR functions and organization's overall practices and procedures.
5. To measure statutory compliances of HR activities as per law and other relevant agencies.
6. To explore the areas for saving personnel costs and expenses.
7. To provide feedback on better areas of performance and areas that needs improvement.
8. To identify HR areas that requires research and development inputs.
9. To recognize better performance of HR personnel through rewards.

(E) Nature of Human Resource Audit:

The nature of Human Resource Audit has been stated as follows:

1. Human Resource Audit, generally, gives feedback about HR functions not only to operating mangers, but also to HR department.
2. Basically, audit is an overall quality control and check the HR activities in a public organisation.
3. Human Resource Audit also helps clarify organisational and management goals.
4. It is used as a tool for review of the effectiveness of human resource practices.
5. It also helps the management of the organisation to evaluate how well its policies are going and identifies trouble areas that require particular attention.

(F) Advantages/Benefits of HR Audit:

K. Aswathappa has explained ten benefits resulting from Human Resource audit.

These are:

(1)   Clarification of the HR department duties and responsibilities.

(2)   Ensuring timely compliance with legal requirements.

(3)   Creation of increased acceptance of the necessary changes in the HR department.

(4)   Stimulation of uniformity of HR policies and practices.

(5)   Encouragement of greater responsibility and professionalism among members of the HR department

(6)   Identification of the contributions of the HR department to the organisation.

(7)   Improvement of the professional image of the HR department.

(8)   Finding solution of critical personal problems.

(9)   Reduction of HR costs through more effective personnel procedures.

(10)   Also review of the department information system.

(G) Need for Human Resource Audit:

According to Yoder, the need for personnel audit is largely influenced by several conditions.

Some of these are:

(1)   **The Number of Employees:** Very small units, because of the very small number of persons they employ, require comparatively little in the way of a formal audit.

(2)   **Organisational Structure:** Continuing feedback is facilitated if an organisation has a personnel department.

(3)   **Communication and Feedback:** An effective two-way communications system often reduces the need for a formal audit.

(4)   **Location and Dispersion:** The need for a formal audit is directly related to the number of isolated plants.

(5)   **Status of an Industrial Relations Manager:** If he participates in the top management plans, reports, discussions and decisions, the need for a formal audit may be less frequently felt.

(6)   **Administrative Style:** The greater the delegation of authority and decentralisation of power, the greater the value of a regular and formal audit.

(H) Scope of Human Resource Management Audit:

Organizational practices regarding the subject matters of HR audit may vary.

However, a comprehensive scope of HRM audit includes all aspects of HRM which are as follows:

1.   HR strategies and policies,

2.   HRM functions,

3.   HR compliance, and

4.   HR climate.

1. HR Strategies and Policies:

The starting point of HRM audit should be an evaluation of HR strategies and policies and the way these are in tune with those of the organization. For formulating HR strategies and policies, it is essential that the objectives of HRM functions are clearly defined. The audit may evaluate the extent to which various HR strategies and policies have been formulated and what their qualities are.

Various HR strategies and policies may be audited by evaluating their:

(i)   Consistency with the organizational objectives, strategies, and policies;

(ii)   Consistency with the environment;

(iii) Appropriateness in the light of organizational resources;

(iv)   Appropriateness in the light of time horizon; and

(v)   Workability.

2. HRM Functions:

The major drive of HRM audit is on evaluation and review of various HRM functions relating to acquiring and employing human resources, developing human resources, compensation management, integration and maintenance of human resources, and industrial relations.

The audit should measure and evaluate these functions in the following context:

(i)   The type of HRM functions performed;

(ii)   The degree to which these functions are related to HRM objectives; and

(iii) The degree to which these functions are performed effectively.

3. HR Compliance:

HR compliance refers to the adherence to various HR strategies and policies by line managers and adherence to legal requirements.

In this context, evaluation revolves around the following:

(i)   The extent to which line personnel adhere to various HR policies in dealing with personnel working under them; and

(ii)   The extent to which there is compliance with the legal requirements as provided under various legal Acts relevant for management of human resources.

4. HR Climate:

Quality of HR climate has important impact on motivation, job satisfaction, morale, and performance of human resources.

HR climate can be evaluated by various outcomes which are as follows:

(i)   Degree of employee turnover,

(ii)   Degree of employee absenteeism,

(iii) Degree of accidents,

(iv)   Status of grievances and disciplinary actions, and

(v)   Findings of attitude and morale surveys.

(I) Importance of Human Resource Audit:

In modern times, personnel and industrial relations audits have been widely accepted as tools with which managers can control the programmes and practices of the personnel and industrial relations department.

The importance of personnel audit has increased in recent years because of the following reasons:

(1) A change in managerial philosophy and theory, as a result of which a management now feels that employees' participation in the activities of an organisation, and their identification with it, have a tremendous influence on the working of that organisation.

(2) The changing role of the government, which intervenes more often and more extensively now, to control manpower management by an organisation with a view to protecting the interests of the employees, providing them with better working conditions and ensuring their economic security.

(3) The increasing role played by trade unions and their strength, as a result of which they often question managerial competence in industrial relations.

(4) The rising wages, changes in the skills of technical and professional workers, and the increasing expenditure incurred on the industrial relations department — these are the factors which have influenced and encouraged the trend in favour of a personnel audit.

(J) Process of Human Resource Audit:

1. **Determining the Scope and Type of Audit:** Since HR is a very wide field, the company may either choose to conduct a comprehensive review of all HR functions or it may decide to review a few specific areas as it deems necessary. For example, a company may choose to review only the policies and procedures related to recruitment, selection and orientation policies.

2. **Determining the Audit Method:** HR audits are usually conducted by using a questionnaire that provokes information about the relevant HR areas. The audit may also be conducted by interviewing managers and employees of the HR department to analyze how well they have understood the company's policies and how efficiently these policies are being implemented. When using a questionnaire, care should be taken to design it in such a way that it elicits all necessary information regarding the areas to be audited.

3. **Data Collection:** This step includes the actual process of collecting data about the organization and its HR practices. Information is collected by using the questionnaire and by interviewing relevant HR personnel about the HR procedures and policies being used in the company.

4. **Setting the Standards:** To assess the efficiency of HR functions, the information collected has to be compared with some pre-determined standards. These standards have to be pre-set and any acceptable level of discrepancies should be specified clearly. Comparing the actual results with the standards will give an idea about the efficiency with which the HR functions are being performed.

5. **Feedback about the Results:** After collecting information and comparing the results, the audit team summarises the findings and provides feedback to the company's HR personnel and senior management in the form of an audit report.

   The results of the audit should be discussed with the employees of the HR department so that they are made aware of the present condition of the HR functions in the company. Discussion with employees will also throw up new ideas for improving the policies and procedures in future.

6. **Develop Action Plans:** Once the results of the audit are out, this information should be used for improving the working of the HR department. The findings of the audit should be categorised according to order of importance: high, medium and low. The organization should examine the areas of weaknesses as revealed by the audit and find ways to overcome them. Conducting HR audit would serve no practical purpose if no actions are taken.

5.4 HR Shared Services: Concept, Objective, Benefits, Issues creating HR Shared Services

(A) Introduction:

Organisations use shared services as a way of organising their HR activities, typically concentrating administrative activities into a centralised and commonly shared function. The shared service model can help businesses reduce costs, avoid duplication of effort, and allow a greater focus on HR strategy objective

HR shared services typically provide routine administration of HR processes such as recruitment, new starters, payroll, the administration of changes to roles/contracts, process time in organisations where relevant, administration of leavers and absences and/or L&D procurement, although the exact nature of the services.

Shared services is an increasingly common organisational response to creating more efficient service delivery. Costs can be reduced through the economies of scale from centralisation of services. Increased customer focus can lead to better quality outcomes. Technology can offer various routes to user friendly delivery (e.g. call centres, intranets, etc.). Choices, though, have to be made on the nature of the shared services operation and on the relationship between HR and line managers and employees.

(B) Meaning of HR Shared Services:

The key dimension of HR shared service is that the activities involved are available to a number of parties. They are common services. Moreover, the customer defines the level of the service and decides which services to take up. A shared services model presupposes central provision.

A variety of activities can be covered in shared services. These include principally administrative tasks (e.g. payroll changes, relocation services, recruitment administration, benefits administration, company car provision, pensions administration, etc.), but also frequently include providing information and advice, or consultancy and high level professional support.

Human resource is very significant aspect of an organisation and has several functions which are incorporated inside a single power-packed capsule. From recruitment to performance measurement and transition or termination processes, there are many intermediary functions that need to be carried away in highest possible expertise. Basic objective of HR shared services is to achieve the perfect operational effectiveness via organised shift of internal services. Efficacy of HR shared services is visible in middle to large sized enterprises having overseas locations.

(C) Importance of HR Shared Services:

1. For any and every problem, you get solution from recentralized HR functions thereby translating into your one-stop shop. There are various sectors of HR shared services and one of them is Business Transformation. Whether you require a solution in relation with Mentoring Programs or Change Management, you can reach HR Admin which would then redirect you to specific department.

2. HR shared services are more selective and strategic because this department need not has to share the enhanced responsibilities associated with administration. That is why, as and when required, based on priorities, HR shared services undertook selective approach to complete a Job.

3. The HR shared services associate requisite staffing demands after considering the availability of allotted funds. Availability of funds is contrasted with demand for expert services in that business domain and its expected value. After consulting with the specific department, HR Admin forwards the requirements for fresh recruitments.

4. One of the major objectives of HR shared services is to enhance the professional approach and efficiency of various services. Such objectives are realized through streamlining the processes and separating them in particular modules. Modularization of services enhances the efficiency of services because specific actions are aimed at finishing the hands-on objectives of that module thereby reducing the chances of error in decision making or giving order and role play.

5. Motto of HR shared services is to offer improved customer services even surpassing their expectations (in positive sense). As mentoring is an significant feature of HR shared services, fortifying the customer service employees with excellent soft-skill proficiency is where they make the acceptable difference. The competitive age not only demands prompt service delivery but also tactful and polite handling of a crisis situation.

6. Service-level agreements are framed after consultation with legal experts hired by the company and HR shared services play important role in framing them. This helps to keep transparency between the employees and the employers thereby also helps to avoid any legal entanglements in future. Based on internal market system, the shared services also keep records of performance monitoring procedures.

7. The shared services help to keep more transparency in keeping a balance in between the market price of services and monitoring the budgets.

(D) Need for HR Shared Services:

Based on IES research on some fifteen organisations, there seem to be three principal drivers to the introduction of HR shared service. These are:

- cost
- quality
- organisational change.

Organisations feel that shared services can reduce costs by three main means:

1. by cutting staff numbers, through achieving economies of scale
2. by reducing accommodation charges, through exiting some offices/using cheaper accommodation
3. by greater efficiency in what is done and how it is done, through streamlining and simplifying services, and doing them to a consistent, accurate standard. Combining purchasing decisions also offers savings through economies of scale.

Quality can, it is thought, be improved through shared services, both in itself and by HR being more customer focused. This is achieved by:

- being more professional
- achieving greater consistency and accuracy
- being more aware of internal and external best practice
- using better processes to complete work
- delivering on time and to budget.
- discovering what the customer wants rather than deciding what suits the service supplier
- becoming more accessible by operating user-friendly services (longer opening hours or easier means of contact)
- improving the supply of information to customers, both on process and content
- giving better quality support in line with customer needs.

There were four sorts of organisational drivers to setting up HR shared services:

- to be part of a wider business change introducing the concept of 'professional' or functional services
- to achieve a greater degree of structural flexibility to respond to business change
- to improve organisational learning across organisational boundaries
- to allow HR to reposition itself as more strategic; to lessen involvement in administrative trivia.

In most of the circumstances we looked at, technology was usually a facilitator of change rather than a driver in itself. However, some shared service models would not have been possible a few years ago. Technical innovation in communications has enabled far reaching change to take place. Developments include using:

- an organisational intranet to provide information on HR policies and procedures
- PIN number based access to personal information

- sophisticated telephony such as IVR (interactive voice response) to offer callers a choice of options to key into from a voice menu, or distributed call systems allowing callers to be routed to remote locations
- document management systems, eg allowing paper to be scanned so as to feed electronic files, to transfer material electronically, and to permit multiple access by HR staff
- workflow systems that guide and prompt the user as to the next steps to be taken
- standard forms on the intranet that can be electronically completed and despatched.

(E) Benefits of HR Shared Services:

As one might expect, the benefits tend to be those sought by organisations when they introduced their new structures, namely:

1. lower and more transparent costs
2. more efficient resourcing; better career development for HR staff
3. better quality services
4. higher customer satisfaction ratings, through an improved match between customer expectations and service
5. a more integrated 'total solution' approach to problems
6. a more selective and strategic contribution from HR
7. improved cross-group learning, partly through having a common information base, accessible to all
8. better management information, provided more consistently across the organisation as a whole
9. facilitation of corporate investment in computing and communications infrastructure by arguing the case on a collective basis.

(F) Issues creating HR Shared Services

Some problems have already been encountered, but the issues to be faced are more likely to be medium term in nature and more to do with getting the benefits out of shared services without creating other difficulties.

(I) Short-term or Transition Issues:

1. recognising that HR has a number of different customers to be convinced and, in particular, that senior management has to support the concept in theory and practice.
2. understanding that there may be a need for large-scale capital investment to get the right technological infrastructure.
3. being careful to determine the best design and choice of operator: in-house or outsourced (in whole or in part).
4. being wary of IT delivery times, cautious of whether the kit will be fully operational on time and to specification.

5. Neglecting the importance of the knowledge and experience of incumbent administrators in staffing new positions, and undervaluing their work.

6. understanding that by stripping out operational tasks, business-facing HR managers may have lost their raison d'être and found it difficult to concentrate on strategy and change management.

7. recognising that boundary management problems may occur if the service is heavily segmented, e.g. where does policy formation end and implementation begin?

8. anticipating communication difficulties, especially where there are numerous discrete activities, each organisationally separate.

9. Protecting against a lack of effective accountability. HR Managers may be responsible for personnel services, but have no control over the work if it is done in a shared service centre.

(II) Issues for the Longer Term:

1. Ensuring HR makes a strategic contribution in deed as well as words.

2. Aligning HR with the business, whereas at the same time performing the role of 'employee champion' that gives HR its distinguishing value.

3. Determining whether efficient use of resources should be more important than fulfilling customer needs, or vice versa.

4. Delegating work to line managers successfully, not dumping unwanted tasks upon them or asking them to perform activities without training or support.

5. Avoiding the risk of de-skilling some administrative jobs to the point where they become extremely tedious to perform.

6. Identifying difficulties with career development if lower graded staff do not build the expertise that allows them to fill more senior positions later.

7. Ensuring that personnel staff are very reliant on being kept well informed of what is happening on the ground.

8. Determining to whom resources should be allocated, especially in a project organisation.

9. Avoiding the risk that project based staff are ill-attuned to business needs, giving generic rather than specific advice and not seeing the work through to a real conclusion.

10. Knowing the risk of giving too much emphasis to selling products and insufficient attention to the content.

Questions for Discussion

1.   Explain the Emerging Trends in Human Resource Management.

2.   What is Human Resource Information System (HRIS) ?

3.   Explain the Importance of HRIS.

4.   State the Advantages and Uses of HRIS.

5.   Define Human Resource Accounting (HRA). State the Need and Purpose of HRA.

6.   Describe the Various Methods of HRA.

7.   State the Advantages and Limitations of HRA.

8.   What is HR Audit ? State its Objectives and Scope.

9.   Explain the Process of HR Audit.

10. What is HR Shared Services ? State its Need and Importance.

11. Discuss the various Issues Creating HR Shared Services.

12. Write Short Notes:

     (A) Benefits of HRIS.

     (B) Types of Human Capital.

     (C) Importance of HR Audit.

     (D) Benefits of HR Shared Services.

HUMAN RESOURCE MANAGEMENT

MBA : Sem. II

MODEL QUESTION PAPER

(CBC & GS 2019 Pattern)

Time : 2 Hours   **Maximum Marks : 50**

Q. 1 : Explain the Objectives, Scope and Role of HRM.   **[10]**

OR

Q. 1 : Explain the various sources of Recruitment.   **[10]**

Q. 2 : Define Performance Appraisal. Explain the various methods of Performance Appraisal.

OR

Q. 2 : Describe the Grievance Procedure in Indian Industry.   **[10]**

Q. 3 : What is HR Accounting ? State its Advantages and Limitations.   **[10]**

OR

Q. 3 : Define Training. Explain the various Methods of Training.

                                                                      [10]

Q. 4 : Explain the Importance and Process of HRP.   **[10]**

OR

Q. 4 : Explain the various methods of Employee Separation.   **[10]**

Q. 5 : Write Short Notes (Attempt any Two)   **[10]**

    (A) HRM Models.

    (B) Succession Planning.

    (C) Benefits of Training.

    (D) HR Shared Services.

✷✷✷

PRAGATI BOOKS

Head Office : Abhyudaya Pragati, 1312 Shivaji Nagar, Off J.M. Road,

Pune : 411005 (Maharashtra) Ph.020-25512336/7/9

Email : niralipune@pragationline.com; marketing@pragationline.com

Website: www.pragationline.com   Also find us on www.facebook.com/niralibooks

---

MBA (Semester-II)
Compulsory Generic Core Course Subjects

- Marketing Management
- Financial Management
- Human Resource Management
- Operations and Supply Chain Management

BRANCH

Dhayari (Pune) : Surve No. 28/27, Near Asian College, Dhayari, **Pune :** 411041
(Outstation)   Tel : (020) 24690204 • Email : bookorder@pragationline.com

Mumbai : Rasdhara Co-op. Hsg. Soc. Ltd. 'D' Wing Ground Floor, 385, S.V.P.
Road, Girgaum, **Mumbai** 400004, Tel: (022)23856339/23869976
• Email :niralimumbai@pragationline.com

Pune City : 119, Budhwar Peth, Jogeshwari Mandir Lane, **Pune :** 411002
(Local)   Tel: (020) 24452044, 66022708
• Email : niralilocal@pragationline.com

MARKETING REPRESENTATIVES

Ahemednagar, Aurganabad : **Mr. Raju Shaikh** •Mob. +91 9850547359
• Email : niraliahmednagar@pragationline.com

Nashik : **Mr.Parag Ghamandi** •Mob. +91 9850490869
• Email : niralinashik@pragationline.com

❖ ❖ ❖